*GOD'S
REACH FOR
MAN*

Books by

ALICE BISHOP KRAMER
and
ALBERT LUDLOW KRAMER

THE LIFE IN THE VINE

A manual for those who are searching for God, and for those who have practical problems.

Price 75 cents postpaid

THE UNLOCKED DOOR

Showing the way of philosophy, psychology and of Christ.

Also "Practical Preaching."

Price one dollar postpaid.

The above are published by Fleming H. Revell Company, 158 Fifth Avenue, New York City.

I BRING YOU JOY

Including "A Business Man's Search for God," and "How He Found Him."

Published by A. Ludlow Kramer,
Westbury, Long Island

Price 50 cents postpaid.

THE WAY

Selections from the Scriptures showing The Way to union with God.

Published by the American Tract Society,
7 West 45th Street, New York City.

Price one dollar postpaid.

All of the above can be obtained through any bookstore.

GOD'S REACH FOR MAN

By

ALICE BISHOP KRAMER

ALBERT LUDLOW KRAMER

"I have stretched out my hand, and no man regarded."

"I have loved thee with an everlasting love: therefore with loving kindness have I drawn thee."

"Behold, I stand at the door and knock."

"Are not these evils come upon us because our God is not among us?"

A. LUDLOW KRAMER, PUBLISHER
425-435 EAST 24TH STREET
NEW YORK CITY

PRINTED IN THE UNITED STATES OF AMERICA
BY J. J. LITTLE AND IVES COMPANY, NEW YORK

FOREWORD

This book is both condensed and repetitious. We have tried to concentrate and repeat Truth.

Presenting Truth is like photographing a person from different points: no two pictures are exactly alike.

Some of the sections may not present that which seems to be a good likeness. If they do not, it may be due to our faulty use of words, or because the same words often mean different things to different people. This is the reason for much theological controversy. Words *are* tyrannous.

We are not conscious of having written anything which is not known to many children of God. We have however attempted to present a simplified theology with a simplified terminology.

This has involved intellectual labor, because God has not used us as a "pen." It has been necessary for us to receive, understand, and assimilate before we could "give forth." We are grateful that through "lowly listening," He has often "established our thoughts."

Jesus tells us that which we ought to be. He devoted even more time to telling us *why* we should BE and *how* to be it. We have tried to follow His example in emphasizing the fruits and gifts which He offers us, and in showing *how* we can be like Him and be united with Him.

The division into parts is more or less arbitrary and is for the convenience of the reader.

A. B. K. and A. L. K.

Westbury, Long Island, New York.

CONTENTS

PART I.

1.

What is truth?

Truth must be eternal—unchangeable.

There is therefore no such thing as a new truth. When we discover something which is new to us, we have merely discovered more of the truth.

2.

Truth is indivisible.

If we subtract from or add to truth it is no longer truth.

That which is nine-tenths true may be more subtly false than a lie.

The addition of the least falsity destroys truth.

3.

The Bible is God's progressive revelation of Himself. It is God's expressed thought.

It is that part of truth which man is able to understand and which he needs to know.

God seems to hide Himself only because we are too far from Him to comprehend Him perfectly.

4.

The Bible tells us that much of its revealed truth cannot be understood by natural man.

Our eye cannot understand music, our ear cannot appreciate a sunset. The spiritual must be "spiritually discerned."

We are able to absorb the Word of God only in so far as we are enlightened by the Spirit of God.

5.

In the natural world there are many things we cannot know excepting through experience. The same is true of the spiritual world.

Large portions of the Bible can only be comprehended after we have progressed upon our spiritual journey. They are often descriptions of our experiences.

We penetrate more deeply into truth as we admit more of the Spirit of God into us.

6.

We do not solve anything when we say that the Bible means what it says. Our difficulty is in understanding what it says.

Parts of it are to be taken literally. Parts of it are symbolic. Parts of it are to be taken both literally and metaphorically.

If we have the Holy Spirit as our Guide, He will lead us through all confusion. He will always interpret for us anything which we need to know at the time.

As a general rule the Bible should be taken literally excepting where it is *manifestly* metaphorical or figurative.

7.

"The prophecy came not in old time by the will of man: but holy men of God spoke as they were moved by the Holy Ghost." (2 Peter 1.)

"The Comforter, which is the Holy Ghost, whom the Father will send in my name, He shall teach you all things, and *bring all things to your remembrance, whatsoever I have said unto you.*" (John 14.) (Italics are ours.)

"If any man shall take away from the words of the book of this prophecy, God shall take away his part out of the book of life." (Revelation 22.)

8.

The Bible was written under the direct supernatural guidance of God.

It *is* truth and cannot be divided. If we add to it or subtract from it, it becomes irrational.

Our beliefs are often false because we do not believe enough.

We do not have to accept its teachings blindly. We can always prove truth for ourselves.

9.

The Bible describes life in a "new country"—the invisible Kingdom of God. It tells us we can "go there" in this life if we comply with the conditions.

When we fulfill the conditions, we find ourselves actually experiencing new life.

We cannot attain truth and new life merely by talking and reasoning about them.

We must "do the thing."

We must take the way.

We must not try to make the Bible agree with our preconceived opinions.

We must not try to fit it into scientific theories.

We must not interpret it according to our wishes.

We must empty our minds and search the Bible for truth.

It is difficult for most of us to believe the promises of the Bible because of their simplicity and vastness.

If we will not believe until we understand, we cut ourselves off from the experience which enables us to understand.

Truth is dogmatic. Compromise destroys it. Sometimes truth must tear its way through our stubbornness.

God is Spirit.

We have a body made of matter. We are flesh and blood.

Correspondence between God and man is difficult. Our senses are limited. We cannot see God with our eyes. He cannot "appear" to us.

We are of a lower order. God has life—*is* Life—
and dwells in light, that is inaccessible to our senses.

13.

Because of our limited senses, minds, and imagina-
tions, it is impossible for us to imagine the "appearance" of God.

"Thou canst not see my face: for there shall no man
see me, and live" (Exodus 33).

Concentration on pictures of Jesus Christ is dangerous. It sometimes like crystal gazing results in self-
hypnosis and delusion.

We must think of Him as Spirit and worship Him
as Spirit.

14.

God created man a living soul in His *image*.

He created man *potentially* like Himself—potentially good, loving, wise, and powerful.

The spiritual seed is in man when he is born, as the
oak is in the acorn, but it is dormant—"dead."

Man is born of the earth, earthy. (1 Corinthians
15.)

Only God can quicken the dead. Only He can call
those things which be not as though they were.
(Romans 4.)

15.

The natural man lives in that which is evil—darkness—to God.

God sees us in the darkness. He is with us in the
darkness. "His eyes are in every place" (Proverbs 15).

Man's eyes are so "dull" that it is impossible for him to see God. Like a bat emerging from a dark pit, he is blinded by an excess of light.

16.

Strictly speaking, no man is solely natural.

We all have at least a dormant spiritual seed *in* us, and God is working *upon* us.

We speak of natural man to distinguish him from the man born into the spiritual life by the supernatural action of God.

17.

If evil did not exist man would be innocent, but he would not be virtuous. We acquire strength only as we overcome.

If man is to become like God, it is necessary that he be free. Of every tree in the garden thou *mayest* freely eat.

As a consequence of man's freedom, the innocent sometimes suffer because of the guilty.

God cannot prevent this suffering without destroying the freedom of man. If man were not capable of baseness, he would not be capable of loyalty and chivalry.

18.

"I form the light and create darkness; I make peace and create evil." (Isaiah 45.)

"I have created the smith that bloweth the coals in the fire, and that bringeth forth an instrument for his

work; and I have created the waster to destroy."
(Isaiah 54.)

Darkness is the absence of light; light exists by contrast with darkness.

We have understanding only as we come out of ignorance into wisdom.

We have virtue only as we overcome evil.

"Jesus being full of the Holy Ghost returned from Jordan, and was *led by the Spirit* into the wilderness."

He was victorious. "I have overcome."

19.

Below us are the mineral and vegetable kingdoms. As natural men—unregenerate men—we belong to the animal kingdom. We are sub-men. The spiritual kingdom—the Kingdom of God—is above us.

The mineral is dead to us. The vegetable is dead to the animal. We are dead to the spiritual kingdom. Christ spoke of us as dead.

20.

The mineral must die—disintegrate—before it is changed into the vegetable kingdom.

The vegetable must die before it is by metabolism transformed into the animal kingdom.

We cannot grow from the animal kingdom into the spiritual kingdom.

The natural man must be willing to die to the nature with which he is born before he can be converted into the spiritual kingdom.

No form of life can rise to a higher one excepting through death. We must lose our limited mortal life if we would gain a higher eternal life.

When man is willing to lose his mortal nature, God will cause the seed of spirituality in him to sprout.

Through this crisis, man ceases to be a sub-man and becomes a son of God. He is "born anew"—"born from above." He becomes a "new creature" and "puts on immortality."

Man cannot accomplish this himself. It is an act of creation.

22.

The continuity of our physical and mental life may hide our rebirth from the uninitiated.

The survival of our physical appearance, of our consciousness, and of our subconscious mind and memory, tend to disguise the fact that there has been a new creation—a spiritual one.

23.

As merely natural men, we have vast potentialities for evil. The best of men, under frustration, may sink lower than animals.

The worst of men may, after they have been born into the Kingdom of God, rise to perfection by the renewing of their minds and hearts.

24.

We learn about God from the Bible and from our experiences with Him.

We learn that the universe is built upon a spiritual —a moral—foundation.

We learn that we are not judged by our physical or intellectual attainments. We learn that these are "foolishness" to God.

25.

There is no conflict between religion and science as long as they stay on their own plane—in their own territories.

Religion deals with the Kingdom of God and its relation to natural man.

Science deals with nature and natural man.

We can be interested in both religion and science; but if we would avoid confusion, we must recognize their boundaries.

26.

Through science, we learn of natural phenomena, attempt to classify them, and call the result "natural law."

Through the Bible we learn something of spiritual phenomena. We learn that they supersede natural phenomena, and that a continuous influence is exerted by the spiritual world over the natural world.

The natural is that which we think we understand. The supernatural is that which we do not understand until we are spiritually enlightened.

27.

We often call the usual—natural, and the unusual—supernatural.

That which seems supernatural to one man is natural to another.

The wise man is impressed by the usual. The shallow man is impressed only by the unusual.

Discussions as to how God performs that which we call miracles implies that we think we understand that which we call natural, and is a manifestation of our egotism.

When we are filled with the Spirit of God, the supernatural becomes supremely natural, and the "irrational" gloriously rational.

28.

We regard it as "natural" that God should have made man out of the dust of the ground. When He makes lice out of the dust of the ground (Exodus 8) we call it a "miracle."

We regard it as natural when He makes wine out of the earth through the vine by a complicated process. When He made wine directly out of water (John 2) we call it His "first miracle."

The birth of Christ as directly conceived by God from a virgin has been a stumbling block only because it was unusual.

29.

Natural man's heart is evil from his youth (Genesis 8).

We are conceived in sin and molded in iniquity (Psalm 51).

To God we are all as unclean things, and our righteousnesses are as filthy rags (Isaiah 64).

If we compare ourselves with others about us we are unwise (2 Corinthians 10).

30.

As long as natural man has evil in him—as long as he is potentially evil—as long as he is not *filled with good*—he *is* evil.

Many whom we call good are not so to God.

He says to those who call "Lord, Lord," but who will not commit themselves to Him: "Bind him hand and foot, and cast him out into the outer darkness."

31.

Christ "knew what was in man."

He knew Peter better than Peter knew himself.

We do not understand life or know ourselves unless we understand that as natural men we are walking in spiritual darkness.

God tells us that our life is built upon sand until we are reborn and filled with His Spirit.

It is when we realize the invincible power of sin over us that we are ready to receive the overcoming power of God.

PART II.

32.

The kingdom of heaven is *at hand*. It is all about us. It is not merely imminent. It is present.

"If I with the finger of God cast out devils, no doubt the Kingdom of God *is come* upon you." (Luke 11.) (Italics are ours.)

"There be some standing here which shall not taste of death, till they see the Kingdom of God." (Luke 9.) "The Kingdom of God *is come* nigh unto you." (Luke 10.) (Italics are ours.)

God dwells in this "new country"—this "heavenly country." It is His Kingdom.

33.

In God's Kingdom there is a new state of life— a more abundant life—a life with new power and love. There is more abundant light—new understanding.

There is a "new language" in the Kingdom of God. The meaning of the Word can be learned only by the teaching of the Holy Spirit.

"In Him are hid all the treasures of wisdom and knowledge" (Colossians 2).

God understands man's limitations.

He understands man's ignorance, stupidity, lack of imagination, fear, cruelty, greed and lust.

God does not love any man because he is wise. To Him we are fools walking in darkness. (Ecclesiastes 2.)

God does not love any man because he is good.

God loves us because God *is* love.

35.

When we speak of "finding ourselves," we mean finding our "best self." This best self exists in us only potentially.

We are really, consciously or unconsciously, looking for God to re-create us.

Nature accomplishes her purposes through hunger and thirst.

Spiritual hunger and thirst lead us to God. They are *of* God.

God is always drawing us to Himself.

The Light will shine through every opened door.

36.

It is important for us to realize that the word "death" is used in three different ways in the Bible.

There is our physical death.

There is the death of self when we commit ourselves to God. "He that loseth his life for my sake shall find it" (Matthew 10). "Except a grain of wheat fall into the ground and die, it abideth by itself alone; but if it die, it beareth much fruit." (John 12.)

There is spiritual death—the state in which we live as natural or carnal men—as mortal men. "To be carnally minded *is* death" (Romans 8). "The wages of sin is death" (Romans 6). "Let the dead bury their dead" (Luke 9). "Death is swallowed up in victory" (1 Corinthians 15). "We know that we have passed from death to life" (1 John 3).

37.

As natural or carnal men, we are mortal. The result of sin is death.

From God's standpoint we are dead now: we are dead spiritually. "To be carnally minded *is* death." It is darkness. It *is* evil.

God offers us citizenship in the Kingdom of heaven.
He offers to change our heredity.
He offers to change our desires.
He offers to adopt us as His children.
He offers us eternal life—everlasting life with Him.
He offers to recreate us now.
He offers to put His Spirit within us now.
He offers us a new birth now.

38.

If we do not accept God's offer we must abide by the result. The wage—result—is continued "death"— separation from God. We remain in darkness. We remain evil. We continue to groan and travail in pain.

Absorption in matter, or in our senses, or in our

intellectual processes is an opiate which separates us from the reality of our spiritual life.

39.

God's difficulty consists of reaching into a lower order of creation, and raising it to His level.

When man is ready—ripe—willing—God causes him to die to his nature, and to be born into a spiritual nature.

Thereafter, man's existence here is used as a school for the development of a character that will fit him for a higher order.

Unless man experiences newness of life here, he would not be happy in Heaven.

Sin in stupid because it is the resistance which we offer to God's attempts to raise us to His level.

40.

It is difficult for the degenerate man to believe in the happiness of wholesome living, or in the happiness of a cultured and intellectual life.

It is difficult for the intellectual man to believe in the joys of a spiritual life. If he is willing to believe, God will change him and give him the power to experience it.

41.

In order that man might understand, God has used the commandments and the law. These were school-masters to bring us to Him. (Galatians 3.)

He has used persuasion. He has used signs and wonders. He has offered wondrous rewards.

His love has used the rod and the whip. In order that His works should be manifested in man, He has sent warnings and chastenings.

Man often persists in regarding these solely as calamities. He resents them instead of profiting by them.

42.

As natural men we are born with varying degrees of spiritual perception.

Some find it difficult to believe in an invisible God, and in His invisible Kingdom.

The unimaginative have thought that God must operate according to man-conceived "natural law," and have regarded miracles as tricks or coincidences.

They have not understood that the God who created can also repair; or that the God who creates in one way a thousand times, can create in a different way when He chooses to do so.

"God is able of these stones to raise up children" (Matthew 3).

43.

To deter man from living in darkness, God visited "the iniquities of the fathers upon the children, and upon the children's children, unto the third and the fourth generation" (Exodus 34).

If we are filled with bravado and think that we are willing to accept the punishment which our sins will bring upon us, we must still consider whether we are willing to accept the consequences which they may bring on others.

We must ask ourselves whether we are willing to

proceed without God, when we know that abiding in Him may prevent the affliction of our children, or may through intercessory prayer, turn aside suffering from those we love.

44.

The Christian religion is the only one with a Book of prophecy.

The detailed "biography" of Jesus was written hundreds of years before He was born. It begins in the third chapter of Genesis.

The Bible is a guide for those who would know God's plan until *the end*.

The Christian religion is also the only religion which has an empty tomb—a risen Saviour.

45.

God is drawing us to Himself with His everlasting love (Jeremiah 31).

We are consciously or unconsciously searching for Him.

"Ye shall go and pray unto me, and I will hearken unto you, And ye shall seek me, and find me, when ye shall search for me with all your heart" (Jeremiah 29).

We find Him when His down-reach meets our up-reach.

We are the lost sheep looking for the Shepherd.

He is the Shepherd looking for us.

He reveals Himself to us when we are ready to believe, trust and obey.

The penalties for not turning to God are mortality, and the suffering which is inherent in the life of natural man.

Suffering is often a goad to make natural man want to be born into a "better country."

The pains of growth and vicarious suffering are light afflictions compared to the misery inherent in sin.

We sacrifice that which is worth while when we are going away from God.

When we have found God, we realize that "sacrifices" required by Him are always surrendering *less* to gain *more*.

God's love pursues us.

He made us for His own purposes, and we do not find rest until we find Him. (St. Augustine.)

He is not content until we accept His love, understanding and power.

We are not content until we *let go* "our right to ourselves," and recognize His right to us.

God "searches" for man: "Behold I stand at the door and knock."

Man "searches" for God: "To Him that knocketh it shall be opened."

God and man meet when man becomes willing to trust and obey God.

They meet at the Door.

Jesus says: "I am the Door."

He who has always been the Rock, became incarnate so that He could also be the Door.

49.

God "chooses" the humble because only those who are humble are teachable. "Who humbleth *himself* to behold *the things that are* in heaven, and in the earth!" (Psalm 113.)

Only those who are willing to empty themselves of *their* foolish wisdom can be instructed. "Of such is the Kingdom of Heaven."

God weeps over those who are proud and over those who think they are good. "The publicans and the harlots (who have repented and believed) go into the Kingdom of God before you." (Matthew 21.)

Many are called but only a "few" are willing to be chosen.

50.

As God is omnipotent, omniscient, and omnipresent, and as He is loving and just, we can know that He does not cause or allow unnecessary suffering.

The shepherds in Persia break the leg of a lamb which is apt to stray, put it in a splint, and carry the lamb about with them, for the purpose of teaching it not to wander.

By doing this, they save it from being devoured by wolves, or from dying a lingering death. They save it "from itself," that is, from its ignorant, stupid, unimaginative nature.

God does not punish because He is cruel. He punishes to deter.

We punish ourselves when we break His laws and separate ourselves from Him.

God provides punishment for disobedience so that we will be obedient and share His peace and joy.

52.

The Bible and experience teach us:
That God loves us.
That He will forgive us.
That He does not want us to suffer.
That He will allow us to go through any mental or physical agony if it is necessary to save us.

53.

We are pitiful creatures to God. We are like sheep who have gone astray, or like chicks who are lost from their mother.

The worst thing that could happen to us would be that our good health, riches, position or comparative goodness would cause us to be satisfied to remain as we are.

It is better for us to endure sickness, poverty, or other "afflictions" than that we should fail to be born into the Kingdom of God.

We are often so filled with ego, that God cannot refrain from using the whip if He would save us from the dark pit.

Periods of financial difficulties, or of illness often have a great purpose behind them.

A few extra dollars a month, or the cessation of pain, often cause a "penitent" to stray again toward the precipice. Our vows tend to vanish with our sorrows.

"The sow when she is full knows not her master; but when she is hungry she makes a noise; and being again fed, is silent." (Apocrypha: Barnabas 9.)

It is better that a man be born blind than that the works of God should not be manifested in Him.

When He was on earth, Jesus used sickness to draw men, women and children to Him. He is still doing so.

"She is not minded to repent . . . Behold I cast her into a bed." (Revelations 2.)

His great desire is to bring us to a simple, childlike faith. When we believe, trust and obey Him, He often cures us supernaturally in order that we may be more closely bound to Him.

Like an earthly parent, God often has to restrain His generosity for our sakes.

It is essential that we frequently ask Him to search

our hearts, and that we listen to that which He has to say to us. If we do not do these things, He may have to send afflictions to us in order to induce us to do so.

He knows the joy He has in store for us, and His loving hand will lay stripes on our back if it is necessary to do so in order that we may be brought to Paradise.

We do not understand the nature of God when we think of the bruises we receive as His "wrath" (as "wrath" is understood by the man in the street).

We do not have to stay in the darkness. He wants us to come into the Light and share His peace and joy.

PART III.

57.

Philosophy tells us to "know ourselves"; psychology tells us to "see ourselves as we are"; and the man of the world knows it is essential that he be "honest with himself."

When we succeed in obeying these injunctions even partially, we know that natural man is filled with selfishness and conceit.

They are at the root of even his kindness, and he often "loves" because he wants to be loved.

He usually has the traits he dislikes in others.

58.

"We cannot see the forest if we are too close to the trees."

We cannot see ourselves fully—we are too close to ourselves.

We do not want to see ourselves. Our ego covers us with a "smoke screen."

We tend to see ourselves as we would like to be.

Our bodies are meant to be temples of the Holy Spirit.

They are often obvious or gilded pigsties.

They are cleansed as we ascend out of the animal kingdom—as we leave our human nature behind us.

The conceit and selfishness of our human nature are the chains that keep us earth-bound.

60.

If we fail to ascend, God may give us a flick with the whip.

If we do not heed Him, He may use the rod. "If thou beatest him with the rod, he shall not die."

When we find God and eternal life we rejoice that He did not spare us.

"Whom the Lord loveth he chasteneth" (Hebrews 12).

"As many as I love, I rebuke and chasten" (Revelations 3).

If we do not recognize the hand of God in our chastenings, and profit by them, worse things will befall us.

61.

No one can be selfless until he has found God and is filled with Him.

Until then we are occupied with our problems—self-centered. Introspection and analysis generally make us more unwholesome.

Asking God to show us ourselves as He sees us always provides us with a correct diagnosis.

God does not ask us to see and confess our sins to Him for His sake. He already knows them. He wants us to see our sins for our own sakes.

If we are to live up to His standards in the future it is essential for us to see how we have departed from them in the past.

62.

When we have committed ourselves and our problems to God, and know that He is taking care of us as He takes care of the birds and the lilies, we are freed from concentration on self.

When we are released from our own burdens, we are able to help others to a victorious life.

63.

The first step is to know ourselves.

The second step is to forget ourselves.

When we come to know ourselves we want to forget ourselves.

Both steps are necessary.

Self dies when we become Christ-centered. It dies by being denied—renounced.

64.

When we are given even a dim vision of the goodness, love and beauty of God, we abhor ourselves (Job 42).

"Woe is me! for I . . . have seen the King, the Lord of hosts" (Isaiah 6).

"O wretched man that I am" (Romans 7).

"Depart from me for I am a sinful man" (Luke 5).
But He will receive a broken and contrite heart (Psalm 51).

65.

If we succeed in cleaning out ourselves to our own satisfaction, and do not accept God to rule our life, we are in great danger.

"The devil tries the servants of God; and if he finds them empty, he destroys them" (Apocrypha: Hermas 2: 12).

Unless God is given possession, fresh evil will enter into us. "And the last state of that man is worse than the first" (Mark 12).

66.

"I will sprinkle clean water upon you, and ye shall be clean" (Ezekiel 36).

"Though your sins be as scarlet, they shall be as white as snow" (Isaiah 1).

"Their sins will I remember no more" (Hebrews 8).

"Today thou shalt be with me in Paradise" (Luke 23).

67.

"Repent and be baptized everyone of you in the name of Jesus Christ for the remission of sins, and ye shall receive the Holy Ghost" (Acts 2).

"If we confess our sins, He is faithful and just to forgive us our sins, and to cleanse us from all unrighteousness" (1 John 1).

"Whosoever believeth (believes, trusts and obeys) Him shall receive remission of sins" (Acts 10).

When we have repented God forgets our sins. He wants us to do so.

If we concentrate on sin, we magnify its power.

We do best when we keep our faces turned toward the Light.

Planting wheat is the best way of killing weeds in ourselves or others.

Letting in fresh water is better than attempting to purify stagnant water.

69.

It should not take great courage for us to face ourselves if we realize that God is right around the corner willing to forgive and forget.

Forgiveness—the love of God—is one of the two central facts of the Gospel. The other central fact is God's eagerness to make us like Himself.

70.

We are fortunate when our sins are obvious ones.

They are much more difficult to deal with when they are hidden in the subconscious mind. Hate, envy, resentment, and the failure to forgive often devastate our bodies with poison before we are conscious of them.

We are sometimes tempted to hope that the self-righteous will fall into conscious sin.

At all times, and in all places, God has been revealing Himself, and has been giving man understanding, as man was able to receive it, and to bear it.

In Old Testament times God gave His primitive people detailed directions as to what they should *be* and *do*.

At times His commands seemed "irrational." He wanted His people to trust and obey Him. It was necessary that they should do so that He might lift them to a higher order.

They attained increasing faith through experiences with Him: His promises were always fulfilled.

Sometimes men have so emphasized the justice of God as to minimize His love.

Sometimes they have so sentimentalized His love as to forget His justice.

We must realize that the universe would be chaotic if God did not reward virtue and punish guilt.

God would not be holy—worthy of love and adoration—if He was not just.

Under the old covenant between God and His people, God remitted the sins of those who repented and who offered a substitute to die in their place. "Without the shedding of blood there is no remission" (Hebrews 9).

There was no virtue in the blood of bulls and goats, but God required these sacrifices as symbolic of the sacrifice which He Himself was to make in the person of His Son.

74.

Mortality—death—is an inevitable result of sin.

Jesus died that we might be immortal.

He "bore *our* sins," the "just for the unjust"; He gave His life as a *"ransom* for many."

"The Lord hath laid on him the iniquity of us all." (Isaiah 53.)

He atoned for our sins—as our Substitute.

"He took *our* infirmities, and bore *our* sicknesses." (Matthew 18.) (Italics are ours.)

We are cleansed by His blood.

75.

A righteous judge cannot acquit a guilty man brought before him, even if he would like to do so.

If the prisoner be someone he loves, and if he is really repentant, he can impose a fine, and provide the money for its payment.

God incarnate paid the death penalty for natural man upon the Cross.

Jesus Christ was the lamb without blemish, slain from the foundation of the world, to cleanse us from our sins. (1 Peter 1. Revelations 13.)

He fulfilled the old covenant.

76.

Jesus did not die to propitiate an angry God.

He *was* both God Incarnate and the Lamb.

Jesus, as God, took upon Himself the sins of the world.

God Himself paid the penalty.

When we realize that He died for us it is easier for us to believe that He will take care of us.

77.

We are saved from our state as natural men by the precious blood of Jesus Christ.

He laid the *foundation* for our redemption when He paid the *penalty* for our sins. "Whosoever believeth in Him shall receive remission of sins." (Acts 10.)

Unbelief, disobedience and sin are synonymous terms.

To *believe in Him* is to make an absolute commitment of ourselves and all we have to Him.

We are redeemed from the *power* of sin by His life *if we do so.*

78.

We are saved from mortality by His blood if we *believe* in Him. The word *believe* is translated from the Greek word which means to *have faith,* that is, to *believe, trust* and *obey.* "Belief," without obedience, is pretense.

We are saved by His blood from paying the *penalty for our sins* if we believe, trust and obey Him.

We are redeemed, through His resurrection life, from the *power of sin* if we believe, trust, and obey Him.

He is The Way.

Do we *believe?* Are we doing the works which He

did? "He that believeth on me, the works that I do shall he do also."

79.

Jesus came that all men through Him might believe.

He is God's provision for the redemption of natural man.

By believing, trusting and obeying Him, man is freed from the penalty of having lived in darkness. He is freed finally from mortality.

By believing, trusting and obeying Him, man is enabled to live in the Light.

80.

Jesus came to enable us to do the will of God.

He came to overcome evil, and to enable men to do so.

We are *not* saved by His blood from the penalty of past disobedience unless we are willing to be obedient in the future.

We are *not* by His life given power over evil, unless we are willing to do His will.

We are "saved" when we are rescued from the "old" man and transformed into the "new" man. We are "saved" when we are born again and follow Him in the new life. We are "saved" when we live in His power and walk with Him to the end.

81.

The wages of sin is still death. To remain merely natural man *is* death. "To be carnally minded *is* death."

The penalty for disbelief remains as it always has been. It *is* darkness. It *is* evil. It is continuing the *status quo* until, as mortals, we die.

God never overlooks the penalty: He never takes the unwilling into His Kingdom.

82.

"The Spirit of the Lord will come upon thee, and thou shalt . . . be turned into another man." (1 Samuel 10.)

"Except a man be born again, he cannot see the Kingdom of God." (John 3.)

"Except a man be born of water and the Spirit he cannot enter the Kingdom of God." (John 3.)

83.

Jesus Christ is the only begotten Son of God.

Man is not born a son of God. "They which are the children of the flesh, these are not the children of God." (Romans 9.) We are born "natural" men— potential sons of God.

God's Spirit enters us, regenerates us, and causes us to be actual sons. "As many as received Him, to them gave He power to *become* the sons of God . . . which were born not of the will of man, but of God." (Italics are ours.)

The "old man" passes away and "a new creature" is born. "Instead of the briar shall come up the myrtle tree." (Isaiah 55. 2 Corinthians 5. Ephesians 4.)

God's Spirit is called the Spirit of adoption. (Romans 8.)

When the Spirit of adoption enters into us we have the right to call God—Father. (Romans 8.)

God made man in His image. (*Image* is from *imago*, from the root of *imitari*, to imitate.)

When man is separated from God, he cannot reflect —image—Him.

85.

The new birth is not merely a change from "badness" into "goodness": it is a change from the natural man into the spiritual man. "Change" is an inadequate word for it. "Convert" or "transmute" are better ones.

The statement that we must be born again is a *foundation fact*.

86.

Christianity is the only religion or system that supplies the power to make our ideals real.

It shows how the spiritual forces of Heaven can be brought down to earth and used by man.

It gives us the key as to how we may remain humble though healthy and prosperous. Christ is that key.

PART IV.

87.

In order to help us to conceive of God, Jesus and the Holy Spirit as One, it is useful to make metaphors with the natural world.

We can use the sea as a metaphor.

The ocean, the gulf, and the bay are *distinct*.

They are also *united*—flowing into each other. They are "one body of water."

88.

"God detached from Himself a mysterious Being, another Self, (Christ) who willingly despoiled Himself of His condition as God." (Godet.)

"The Lord said unto the Lord."

"The Holy Spirit is an emanation from the Divine Essence." He is in Himself the Divine Essence. He is God.

The Scriptures often speak of the Holy Spirit in us as Christ in us, or God in us.

89.

When we find God through giving ourselves to Him, and He causes us to be born into His Kingdom, the deity of Jesus is revealed to us.

It cannot be made known to us by another man.

Only God can put this knowledge in our hearts.

"Simon Peter answered and said, Thou art the Christ, the Son of the living God.

"And Jesus answered and said unto Him, Blessed art thou, Simon Bar-jona: for flesh and blood hath not revealed it unto thee, but my Father which is in heaven." (Matthew 16.)

"No man can say that Jesus is the Lord, but by the Holy Ghost." (1 Corinthians 12.)

90.

Jesus was human through His Mother.

Jesus was divine through His Father. He was the only begotten Son of God.

He unfolded His spirituality. We acquire it through adoption.

Jesus is one with us in origin through His Mother. Through His Father He is one with God.

"Ye are from beneath; I am from above." (John 8.)

91.

"Who is a liar but he that denieth that Jesus is the Christ? He is antichrist that denieth the Father and the Son.

"Whosoever denieth the Son, the same hath not the Father." (1 John 2.)

"Beware of false prophets which come to you in sheep's clothing, but inwardly they are ravening wolves.

Ye shall know them by their fruits." (Matthew 7.)

The deity of Jesus is proven by His life, His works and His resurrection.

The deity of Jesus is proven because He *is found* as the living Saviour by millions. His existence is proven daily.

They know that His teaching was of God (John 7), and that it is good tidings of great joy. (Luke 2.)

"If this counsel or this work be of men it will come to naught: But if it be of God ye cannot overthrow it." (Acts 5.)

If you reject the corner stone "The kingdom of God shall be taken away from you," and given to those who will bear fruit. (Matthew 21.)

93.

God caused Himself to be born into a lower order of creation in order to lift it to His Kingdom. "How long shall I be with you? how long shall I suffer you."

"When thou tookest upon thee to deliver man, thou didst not abhor the virgin womb." (Te Deum.)

Christ bore our sinful nature. Our evil was "laid on Him."

As Jesus the man, He was "made sin"; but as God, "sin was not in Him."

Jesus as man, could "do nothing"; but as God, nothing was impossible for Him.

Natural or carnal man can do no more than give his life for his friends. God gave His heavenly life for sinners.

He descended so that we might ascend.

Jesus Christ lifts the veil between God and man.

God reveals Himself to man in the person of Jesus Christ.

Jesus came to identify Himself with man. Through Him, we can become God-centered instead of self-centered.

He inaugurated a new race of men. He lived the life of this new man under conditions in which the old man had failed.

The personification of God's love in Jesus Christ moves us in a way that an incorporeal love could not.

"The God whom we worship is not a God who hides Himself, but one who, in order that men might enter into fellowship with Himself, became incarnate in Jesus Christ."

"In Him dwells all the fulness of the Godhead in a bodily form." (Colossians 2.)

"Being originally in the form of God . . . emptied himself, and took upon him the form of a servant, and was made in the likeness of men." (Philippians 2.)

"God, who commanded the light to shine out of darkness, hath shined in our hearts, to give the light of the knowledge of the glory of God in the face of Jesus Christ." (2 Corinthians 4.)

"Who is the image of the invisible God, the first born of all creation." (Colossians 1.)

"I came out from the Father and am come into the world." (John 16.)

"Before Abraham was, I AM." (John 8.)

"I and the Father are one." (John 10.)

"I am come . . . To do thy will, O God." (Hebrews 10.)

"I seek not mine own will, but the will of him that sent me." (John 5.)

"Not my will, but thine, be done." (Luke 22.)

"He who doeth the will of God abideth forever." (1 John 2.)

97.

We help men by believing in them—by believing in their potentialities.

Christ did not believe in *natural* man.

He "knew what was in man."

He said, speaking of Judas, "one of you is a devil."

Jesus believed in the man who would allow Him to live in him, as He, Jesus, lived in the Father.

98.

"He that believeth in me, believeth not in me, but on him that sent me. And he that seeth me seeth him that sent me. I am come a light into the world, that whosoever believeth on me may not abide in darkness." (John 12.)

"Be not afraid, only believe." (Mark 5.)

"Whosoever liveth and believeth on me shall never die." (John 12.)

"Believe and you pass from death to life." (John 5.)

"That mortality might be swallowed up of life." (2 Corinthians 5.)

99.

"Lord, show us the Father, and it sufficeth us.

Jesus said unto him, Have I been so long time with you, and yet hast thou not known me . . . he that hath seen me hath seen the Father." (John 14.)

PART V.

100.

How can we "find God"?

How can we be "converted" from mortal men into immortal men?

How can we be "born again"?

How can we be "saved"?

Is there anything *we* can do about it? Is there any condition with which we can comply?

This is what thousands of people want to know.

HOW?

There is only one answer although it can be stated in many ways.

101.

"The wind bloweth where it listeth, and thou hearest the sound thereof, but canst not tell whence it cometh, and whither it goeth: so is everyone that is born of the Spirit."

We cannot understand the wind. We cannot understand our natural birth. We cannot understand our spiritual birth.

We must be realists. We must accept them as facts.

If we obey the law of the wind we can use its power. If we obey the law of the Spirit, we are born anew.

Until we *know* that Jesus Christ is God incarnate, we fail to see the unity of the Bible, and much of its contents seem irrational and contradictory to us.

"Ye know him; for he abideth with you, and shall be in you." (John 14.)

How can we *know?*

Jesus answers "If any man willeth to do His will he shall know." (John 7.)

If we are *willing* to believe, God will reveal Truth to us.

When we give ourselves to God, we "find" Him— "meet" Him—"know" Him.

"Thou shalt know that I am the Lord." (Isaiah 49.)

"I will manifest myself unto him." (John 14.)

"He that believeth (trusts and obeys) the Son of God hath the witness in himself." (1 John 5.)

"I will not leave you comfortless: I will come to you." (John 14.)

"He that is of God heareth the words of God: for this cause ye hear them not, because ye are not of God." (John 8.)

We find God when we say the Lord's Prayer and mean it: "Thy Kingdom come, Thy will be done" *in me.*

When we are willing to turn over the control of ourselves to God "something happens." The Spirit of God becomes "nearer than breathing, closer than hands and feet."

We have access to "the secret place of the Most High." We can enter into the "Holy of Holies."

105.

Man's search for God fails until he complies with the condition under which God reveals Himself.

We gain power in the natural world by surrendering to it.

We have the power of God—we have God—when we surrender to God.

In both the natural and spiritual worlds we have the most power when Power possesses us most completely.

106.

When we know that God was in Christ—that Christ was an indivisible part of the infinite God—that He was *in essence* God—that He was rooted in God, and filled with God—most of our difficulties vanish.

"Believing in Jesus Christ" includes "doing God's will." Trusting and obeying Jesus Christ is doing God's will because Jesus Christ is God.

107.

As natural men we cannot obey God's commandment to love Him with all our heart, soul, and mind—to put Him first in everything.

We cannot compel ourselves to do so. Our efforts and our wills utterly fail. It is *not in us to do so*.

The dormant seed of spirituality must be quickened by the entrance of God's Spirit. We must be born anew before we have the power to obey.

We must realize the difference between charming people who are trying to "imitate" Christ, and those who have received the Spirit of adoption and are the children of God.

108.

Believing in Jesus Christ means we are willing to have our will disintegrate and die, and to allow His will to have possession of us.

God puts His spirit within us when we surrender that which we have regarded as our right to ourselves.

We cannot receive—accept—Him as an honored guest. We must commit ourselves to Him as Master.

We must give ourselves to Him. We must be willing to do anything He asks us to do.

He is our Saviour when He is our Lord.

God chooses the "meek" and the "weak" because they are willing to give the control of themselves to Him.

109.

"Except a grain of wheat fall into the earth and die, it abideth by itself alone; but if it die, it beareth much fruit." (John 12.)

"Thou fool, that which thou sowest is not quickened, except it die." (1 Corinthians 15.)

"A new spirit will I put within you." (Ezekiel 36.)

"I will put my spirit upon him." (Matthew 12.)

"It is the Spirit that quickeneth." (John 6.)

His Spirit gives life to our "dead" spirit.

The body of the seed is covered with a waterproof jacket. Its only means of communication with the outside world is through a door called the micropyle.

Through this door it drinks water which causes it to "explode"—to die.

Our will is covered with a jacket of stubbornness, but there is an open door through which we can drink of the living water. "The Kingdom of heaven is like a grain of mustard seed . . . when it is grown, it is the greatest among herbs, and becometh a tree." (Matthew 13.)

Psychologists describe conversion as an explosion. The self-will is shattered—it dies.

We rise from our dead selves to better things.

It is not our sins of the flesh, but our claim of our right to ourselves, that is of the essence of sin.

We can decide to give ourselves to Him in a moment, or we can go through years of indecision.

Jesus came to give us the power to obey.

We can accept Him as our Saviour instantly if we choose to use the power which The Cross and Resurrection make available for us.

Will you do it?

As natural men, we can truthfully say, "I *cannot* transform myself." It is even more true than most of us realize.

We can never truthfully say that we *cannot* believe, trust and obey God. When God commands, He always promises us that He will enable us to obey.

If we give Him possession of us He transforms us.

Failure to give Him possession is always because we *will* not—never because we *cannot*. If we "cannot" because of our obstinacy, we can appeal to God to cure our obstinacy!

113.

Often men and women will not see the necessity of giving control of themselves to God because they do not want to see it.

They persist in believing they can "develop" into new life. They think they can create life.

"The Lord God made . . . every plant of the field . . . before it grew." It is "God who quickened the dead and calleth those things which be not as though they were."

114.

Man is not born again through being carried away by his emotions.

He is not born again because of his intellectual beliefs.

Turning toward God, and practicing His presence are steps on the way; but God does not reveal Himself to us because of our striving. "Our painful labors are unnecessary and fruitless."

God makes Himself known to us, and enters us, when we *yield* to Him.

The secret of our spiritual life is letting God re-create us and develop the new creation.

Surrender centers around our will. Are we willing that our will shall be exchanged for the omnipotent will of God?

115.

In both worldly and spiritual matters, conversation often tends to satisfy us. We must be careful not to use it as a substitute for action.

"*Be* ye." "*Do* ye."

"We must *do* the thing."

We must actually make our commitment; we must actually give ourselves to God; we must actually consent to the death of our will.

We must *let go*.

We must *take the plunge*.

We do best when we do not teach that which we have not experienced. Otherwise we may be "enchanted but unchanged."

116.

"The New Birth:

"Most solemn question that will ever come before us in this life.

"The foundation of all our hopes in the life to come.

"It is the A. B. C. of our blessed hope.

"Nothing will upset false religion like it.

"It will change our thoughts about God and the Bible sooner than anything else.

"I believe it is the greatest blessing that will ever come to us in this life." (Copied from notes of Dwight Moody by permission of his son-in-law and secretary Albert Fitt.)

If we have difficulty in *letting go*—in *taking the plunge*—God will enable us to do so if we appeal to Him.

If we are *willing to be obedient* God will guide us until we are finally brought through the veil to the Holy of Holies.

"If there be first a willing mind, it is accepted according to that a man hath." (2 Corinthians 8.)

If we are not willing, He will make us willing if we want Him to do so with all our hearts.

We can pray our way from vileness to holiness.

If our consciousness of sin is a deep one, and if we are willing that our will shall completely die, our rebirth is a conscious, and sometimes, a dramatic one.

It is always joyous.

If the knowledge of our sinful nature comes to us slowly, and if we surrender our will a bit at a time, we may reach our destination without realizing it immediately.

A plunge into water makes a splash. We can walk into it so slowly as to create hardly a ripple.

A danger of walking in is in thinking that we are completely in when we are not. Both our heart and our head must be surrendered to Him.

To *surrender* and to *believe* mean exactly the same thing.

When we are enlisted under the King of kings, our job is to obey orders.

We are not called upon to solve all the problems of the world: He is solving them.

He is planning the campaign. We can help Him only if we will fulfill the great or small part which He assigns to us.

We must not "confer with flesh and blood," or follow what some one else is doing.

"What is that to you?"

We must follow Him: follow where He leads *us*.

"By faith Abraham went out, not knowing whither he went." (Hebrews 11.)

"Belief"—"Surrender"—"Enlistment" mean:

The surrender of our wills.

The surrender of our ambitions.

The surrender of our objectives.

The surrender of our activities.

The surrender of our opinions (especially our opinion of ourselves).

The surrender of our reasoning.

The surrender of our planning.

The surrender of our natural affinities.

The surrender of our bodies.

The surrender of our passions.

The surrender of our health.

The surrender of all self-effort as to our character (our cleansing and sanctification).

The surrender of our security.

The surrender of our "right to ourselves."

Everything we are and have must be surrendered. He returns to us everything which His love for us will permit us to retain.

121.

Our lives with Christ are incomplete when we do not surrender *all*.

Some of us surrender our hearts but insist upon our opinions.

Some of us surrender our security but worry about our health.

Some of us surrender our cleansing but insist upon our objectives, and so forth.

We must dedicate all and leave all dedicated.

"Oh Lord, take me and keep me."

122.

We are failing in compassion when we fail to make a complete surrender. We cannot feed the hungry in our power, and if we will not deny self so that God can use us, we are allowing them to starve.

Our prayer must be: "help us to want to be like Jesus." When we have a tearful compassion and do not give God possession of us so that He can convert others through us, we are merely sentimentalists.

123.

It is only when we dispossess self and give God possession that we can be always kind and always reliable. It is only then that we can feel and manifest His love and compassion. It is only then that we can have His radiant courage and fortitude. It is only then that we can be heroic enough to wear the world as a loose garment.

124.

We have genius when we are possessed by something outside of ourselves.

St. Paul was the greatest genius of all time. He permanently changed the history of the world.

He was God-filled—God possessed. "It is no longer I but Christ liveth in me."

125.

God does not want us to plan our lives. He wants us to give ourselves to Him and to listen to His plan for us. He will guide us every step along the way— one step at a time.

Sometimes the only thing that is keeping us from knowing Him is our insistence upon our own planning. "Lord what wilt Thou have me do?"

When we are abiding in Him, and need an immediate decision as to any problem, we can flash an inquiry to him. "Before they call, I will answer; and while they are yet speaking, I will hear." (Isaiah 66.)

126.

Jesus Christ is the God-man.

Those who "come to," "believe in," "receive," "abide in" Jesus Christ, perceive God, and are gradually changed into the same image.

We can see Him only dimly, as through dark glasses; but if we keep our face toward Him, we are changed into His likeness (2 Corinthians 3).

"Behold me: because I live." (John 16.)

PART VI.

127.

We should love the world as God made it.
We must hate the world as man makes it.
We must become ashamed of our bondage.

128.

We are drawn to God because He has "set eternity in our hearts."
Consciously or unconsciously we want to be God-like.
Consciously or unconsciously we need Love.

129.

When we oppose the wind and current they exhaust us. They are beneficient when we obey them.
The "terrible God" ceases to be terrible when we hearken to Him. When we cease resisting Him we realize that He is the loving Father.
The Holy Spirit is the "Spirit of Burning" to the impure.
"Disobedience makes a benevolent power our enemy." (Phillips Brooks.)

"Perfect love casteth out fear."

Who has perfect love?

Most of us need "the fear of God in our hearts," that is, we need to fear the breaking of His commandments. "The fear of God is the beginning of wisdom."

In the natural world, fear is "a warning monitor."

The door of eternal life may be opened to us through fear of God who *is* a " terrible God" to those who are unmindful of Him.

We have perfect love only when we are filled with Love—filled with Christ. His perfect love in us casteth out fear.

Psychologists tell us that it is not a difference in intelligence or personality that accounts for man's varying degrees of accomplishment. It has been learned experimentally that it is the difference in man's imagination and power of concentration that are the determining factors.

It should not be difficult in this generation for us to believe in the reality of the unseen. Many of the greatest forces which we are using are invisible.

"Blessed are they that have not seen, and yet have believed." (John 20.)

If we want to become acquainted with anyone in our worldly life, we must spend time with them.

If we want to become acquainted with God, we must spend time with Him, and with His Word which is written for us and to us.

The more we concentrate on God and His Word, the more quickly we will be brought to Reality and Truth.

134.

Our imagination can take us into descending or ascending spirals.

As Shakespeare tells us, if we meditate on sin, we "first endure, then pity, then embrace" it. We descend.

If we commune with God, He brings us to a point of surrendering ourselves to Him. This brings experiences with Him, which in turn gives us more faith to surrender more completely. We ascend.

135.

The telescope and microscope help us to realize the limitations of our senses.

The former shows us dimly something of the greatness of God. The latter shows us the care which He exercises upon the least of His creations.

"Who humbleth himself to behold the things that are in heaven, and in the earth!" (Psalm 113.)

136.

Our senses often deceive us. Our eyes and ears, and our sense of touch and taste, often limit our vision.

Sometimes they lull us to sleep. We use them as

we do drugs and alcohol to "escape" from reality. We drown our conscience by pleasure. "They refused to hearken and . . . stopped their ears, that they should not hear." (Zechariah 7.)

137.

It is no more wonderful to *see* without the eye than to see with it.

We must see through that which we see. We must *perceive*.

As natural men we are the servants of the "actual" —of "facts."

Through union with God (*and only then*) we can use the spiritual—to dominate the actual.

We become realists: we cease to "escape" by being materialists.

138.

We must see through the symbols to reality.

The rock, the open door, and the well of water speak to us.

It is God speaking through them.

139.

As natural men we tend to think of the world as we would wish it to be.

We are not realists. "Hundreds can talk for one who can think. Thousands can think for one who can see." (Ruskin.)

We call ourselves masters of our fate even though we know we can be annihilated at any moment by a germ.

We call ourselves rational even though we think we can walk independently of the Potter, and that as clay, we can mould the clay—can change ourselves.

Jesus Christ was the great realist. "I am come into this world that they which see not might see." (John 9.)

140.

When we use our vision to rise above the actual, we must be sure that we are directing it toward reality—toward God.

If we are walking away from Him, we may find ourselves in a pigsty, or in the company of demons.

All "paths," "gates," "keys" that lead toward Him converge upon The Way of being willing to abandon our wills and give Him possession of us.

141.

If we glorify either our intellect or our scholarship we are making *false gods*.

When we use study as an end in itself, we are "dead" from God's standpoint.

"Accomplishment" may temporarily satisfy our ego, but it means nothing to God if it is not a step on the way to eternal life.

142.

Our intellect should be our tool. When it is worshipped as a god it tends to lose its usefulness.

The "life of reason" may bring us into labyrinths in which we flounder and sink.

If we do not know we are lost—if we think we are unlocking doors when we are not—we lose our sanity.

143.

We can sometimes overcome habits of conduct or thought by "neglecting" them and doing something else; by changing our environment; by being with people; and by "occupational therapy."

Christ deals with causes. All our "complexes" are straightened out "automatically" as His Spirit enters us, and fills us.

144.

The psychiatrist must have a technique in dealing with the problems of individuals. Even so, he must often feel his way. His methods must be more or less experimental.

He should have a great understanding of human nature. He should know the world.

He must be a scientist, and should also be an artist.

To attempt psychological work as an amateur is as dangerous as to attempt surgery.

145.

In ministering to individuals the reborn minister has the Holy Spirit as an infallible Guide.

God knows all the facts and will lead His disciples in dealing with individuals.

He supplies all the necessary technique by establishing our thoughts and directing us as to what we should ask, say and do.

When we give the *control of ourselves* over to God —when we allow Him to *take possession of us*—His wisdom operates through us.

146.

The physician and psychiatrist must diagnose in order to know what to prescribe.

The disciple of Jesus has one remedy for spiritual, mental and physical ills.

His prescription is that we should kneel at the foot of the Cross: that we should present ourselves to God and let Him rule us (Romans 6).

147.

The Christian teacher is hurting the cause of Christ when he turns to psychology and deals with people on the plane of science. It is an admission of failure.

The skepticism of the unbeliever is understandable when he sees that we have not found in Christ an answer to individual problems.

When we go to psychologists, we often show that we are unbelievers in Jesus and the historic church.

148.

There are hundreds of religious, ethical, philosophical and political ideologies.

Christianity is the only one which tells us how we can make our dreams come true.

149.

Psychology teaches us to look at ourselves objectively, but it does not show us how we can do this.

Only man born of the Spirit can look at the "old"—natural—man from a detached point of view.

When we are able to do this, we have attained a power to use our body and brain instead of having them use us.

The Christ in us enables us to handle the mechanical part of ourselves, including our habits. We are no longer controlled by automatism.

150.

Analyzing anyone—examining into that which they are, and why they are as they are, focuses our minds and their minds on the "weeds."

When Jesus was asked "who did sin, this man, or his parents, that he was born blind," He answered "I must work the works of Him that sent me."

We know that everyone is potentially a child of God, and our part should consist of showing them how they can actually become so. Loving them is a "more excellent way." (1 Corinthians 12-13.)

151.

We should allow only God to analyze us. Only He is infallible. Only He can change us. Only He can "garrison" and "sublimate" our imagination.

The regenerate man could not be psychoanalyzed very deeply. The Christ in him would revolt against it. We must see our sins, but we must not live in them.

"Thou only knowest the hearts of the children of men." (2 Chronicles 6.)

There is need in every generation for an exposition of the gospel in terms that are fresh and vital, but we must not be snared by meaningless words.

Much is written on the subject of "spiritual culture" that has no meaning.

Cloudy thinking is often disguised by a clever or fulsome use of words.

"Let no man deceive you with empty words."

If we are fluent of speech it may disguise our stupidity even from ourselves, and make it difficult for us to acquire the humility to learn.

153.

Jesus was crucified by those who were afraid of losing their own power. Many are attempting to dethrone Him for the same reason at the present time.

Unbelief, or "partial belief," in Jesus Christ as God Incarnate, *is* sin. Those who deny the claims of Jesus and at the same time call Him righteous and wise, have a strange idea of righteousness and wisdom.

154.

In speaking of some of the so-called religious sects, we must not express ourselves by saying: "there is good in all of them."

A doctrine that is half true may be worse than one that is wholly false. A doctrine that is nine-tenths true may be the most vicious of all. The innocent can be given a poison so mixed with sugar that those who do not understand will drink it to their death.

There are many "false prophets," "blind leaders of the blind" and "wolves in sheep clothing," masquerading under the name of Christianity.

"They have taken away my Lord."

PART VII.

156.

Self-assertion is sin. It is the "original" sin. It is the mother of sins.

Adam refused to take orders from God. He believed in himself.

He refused to remain connected with the Source. He "fell."

157.

The popular Greek philosophy, since known as Hellenic, is Adamic.

The Greeks in general believed in themselves, asking "help" from their gods.

Through the centuries many sects with different terminologies have been followers of the Adamic philosophy.

158.

Emerson's early philosophy of self-reliance (which he repudiated later), "New" Thought, and the "religious sciences" are Hellenic—Adamic.

They are the greatest enemies of Christianity in America.

They account for much of our conceit and boastfulness.

159.

Hellenism emphasizes that man is not using the power he should use. It teaches that man can generate power within himself.

Christianity agrees that man is not using his available power, but it teaches that the reason for this is because he is not connected with the Source.

160.

Hellenism is a philosophy of self-sufficiency.

Christianity teaches that we have no power apart from God, but that we can do "all things" if we are united with Him. It teaches that "our sufficiency is of God."

161.

The Adamic philosophy separates man from God, and develops conceit. Chistianity develops humility and unites man with God.

The Adamic philosophy makes man selfish. Christianity makes him unselfish.

162.

The Adamic philosophy depends on the knowledge man can acquire without God. Christianity opens to him the treasures of wisdom and knowledge that are in God.

The Adamic philosophy is still listening to what the

serpent said to Adam: "open your eyes—believe in yourself—and ye shall be as gods."

John the Baptist said: "A man can receive nothing except it be given him from heaven." Jesus said: "Without Me, ye can do nothing."

163.

Socrates did not believe in the popular Greek philosophy. He wished that "someone would come down from the skies" and tell man that which he could not know of himself.

Israel, who knew God, said: "O that Thou wouldst come down."

Christ came, died and rose again. He says: I am your contemporary. You need only believe in me and I will save and lift you. You no longer need wait for God's voice in the cloud or in the burning bush. Believe in Me, and I will send my Holy Spirit to you.

164.

"Man can mould his own soul, mind and body." "He can change his own consciousness."

"Man's dominion lies within his own mentality."

These are the teachings of "New Thought" and the "religious sciences." They are false. They are Adamic.

"As a man thinketh in his heart, so is he" (Proverbs 23) means that a man is no better than the thoughts in his heart. It does *not* mean that he can change himself by his own thinking.

"Thou fool, that which thou sowest is not quickened, except it die." (1 Corinthians 15.) When we are willing to die to self, Christ comes into us, and gives us power to do so.

165.

We sometimes think we have discovered something new whereas we have only invented a new name for something that is very old.

When we examine the substance of many "new" religions, and of many political and economic systems, we find that they are indeed as "old as the hills."

"New" Thought is a return to living "under the law"—living by our own powers. Jesus came because teachings like those of "New" Thought failed.

"Christ is become of no effect unto you, whosoever of you are justified by the law; ye are fallen from grace." (Galatians 5.)

166.

Those who are following the Hellenic philosophy sometimes have a clear conception of all that we *should* be. Sometimes they have a greater faith in that which we *can* be than many so-called orthodox Christians.

They fail because they have a wrong conception as to *how* their vision is to be realized.

167.

Christ will not come and dwell in the old man.

If new wine is put into an old bottle, the bottle will explode.

It is only when we are regenerated that we are capable of standing the "chemicalization" set up by the entrance of Christ.

It is only when we are purified by Him that we can be filled with Him.

The "fire" of God would consume unregenerate man. (Exodus 19.) "Let not God speak with us lest we die."

168.

God often saves us by letting us first learn the suffering inherent in disobedience. He allows us through experience to learn to fear separation from Him. "Come and let us return unto the Lord, for He hath torn and He will heal us." (Hosea 6.)

To the self-satisfied, He says: "Woe to them that are at ease in Zion." (Amos 6.)

To the "mighty," He says: "Neither shall the mighty deliver himself." (Amos 2.) "Though thou exalt thyself as the eagle, and though thou set thy nest among the stars, thence will I bring thee down." (Obadiah.)

To all who will not accept Him to rule their lives, He says: "The Lord . . . will not at all acquit the wicked . . . He knoweth them that trust in Him." (Nahum 1.)

"I caused it to rain upon one city, and caused it not to rain upon another city . . . and the piece whereupon it rained not withered." (Amos 4.)

169.

The lighting of a whole city depends on two wires being connected.

"Seek ye first the Kingdom of heaven"—connect yourself with the Source—and power, understanding and the fulfillment of your practical needs will "automatically" follow.

170.

From the beginning God knew man would be a failure if he was disconnected with the Source—Himself.

God often has to let man experience the truth of this. "It is impossible for anyone to begin to learn what he thinks that he already knows." (Epictetus.)

Often when man learns for himself something about his capacity for evil, he is prepared to return to God, and learn of the glorious destiny that awaits him when he achieves union with his Creator.

171.

Since the dawn of history, under every conceivable form of government, man has tried to change himself, and rule himself, and has failed.

Our national motto is "In God We Trust." Our only salvation—rationally, scripturally and historically —is to realize our dependence on Him and to return to Him.

Without God, we are like herd animals and will continue to swing from conceit to fear.

172.

To affirm that we *are*, that which we *are not*, is dangerous. In deceiving ourselves as to that which we are, we violate all the conclusions of experience, philosophy, psychology and the scriptures.

To affirm that we are spirit when we are flesh and blood; that we are children of God when we have not been born anew; that we are well when we are ill; that we are rich when we are poor is a form of self-stimulation, the reaction from which may be devastating.

173.

If "affirmations" as to that which we *are not* do not deceive us, they are useless. If we are successful in deceiving ourselves we may be on a road to demon-possession—hallucinations, and insanity.

Jesus taught that the leopard *cannot* change his spots, nor the Ethiopian his skin, and that we *cannot* add one cubit to our stature.

174.

Many people do not find God because they are looking for a god who does not exist.

If they are looking for a god who is merely principle, or for a god who does not recognize the existence of sin or sickness, or for a god who has merely a sentimental love for them, they will not find Him.

They will not find a god who is merely a teacher, or one who will be merely *useful* in helping them in *their* plans, or in strengthening *their* wills.

They will not find a god interested only in their physical health, or in their worldly needs.

God will not take the burden of our problems unless we give ourselves to Him.

We commit suicide when we refuse union with Him.

176.

Man is free to choose between God and Adam. This is the area of our free-will.

God does not want puppets. He does not want to force men to do His will. Neither God nor man can make loving men by legislation.

God *draws* us with His love. "Whosoever *will*, let him take the water of life freely." (Revelation 12.)

If we do not obey God, He may put pressure upon us. It is our resisting this pressure that causes our pain. When we have turned toward Him, He often runs to meet us and carries us over the last fences. (Luke 15.)

177.

When we come to realize the obstinacy of man we no longer think there is a surplusage of suffering in the world.

We wonder at the patience of God.

178.

"I will stretch out my hand." (Exodus 3.) (Jeremiah 51.) (Ezekiel 14.)

"His hand is stretched out, and who shall turn it back?" (Isaiah 14.)

He loves us with a "love that will not let us go."

"In youth I sought a far famed flower rare
And searched in vain through every clime and state,
Till when I wandered home in dark despair
I found the flower by my garden gate."

179.

God asks us to "let go."
We "hang on."
Our "striving" is often only our resistance to that which He is asking us to do.

180.

"Jeshurun waxed fat . . . then he forsook God." (Deuteronomy 22.)

The so-called prosperity of natural man is often darkness, and God sometimes permits it to continue until man experiences the stumbling inherent in darkness.

Although they would not so state it, there are those who believe that some people need union with God, but that they themselves can safely remain independent of the Source.

This contradicts the core of the teachings of Jesus: that all men are lost until they are connected with God.

181.

God allows us to be bound by sin, sickness or poverty if it is necessary to make us value the liberty which He offers us.

He "bringeth out those which are bound" into a victorious life if they are willing to obey.

It is difficult for some of us to reconcile God's chastisements with His love for us. It is difficult for some of us to understand a God who says: "I form the light and create darkness; I make peace and create evil." (Isaiah 45.)

When we read: "I will cast her into a bed" (Revelations 2), some of us are apt to declare that we do not want that kind of love even although we would afflict our own children to prevent them from falling into everlasting darkness.

To God, a thousand years are as a day and He will cause (or "permit") us to suffer for part of a "day" to bring us out of the "horrible pit."

"As a man chasteneth his son, so the Lord thy God chasteneth thee." (Deuteronomy 8.)

"Thou . . . hast loved them as Thou has loved Me." (John 17.)

183.

There is nothing man can do to upset God's plans.

If we stay His chastening rod in one direction, He may wield it in another.

Patching people up mentally, physically or financially *may* only prolong their journey to Him.

184.

Mental therapy, medicine, surgery and alms-giving are unavailing if men stay separated from the Source.

God can create new germs and withdraw intelligence from those who will not accept Him and His righteousness.

Our stubbornness often causes God who is love to put pressure upon us.

185.

"If ye walk contrary unto me . . . I will bring seven more plagues upon you." (Leviticus 26.)

There are a thousand ways in which God can put pressure upon us. His love for us insists upon His doing so. His nature (Love) would not permit Him to do otherwise.

Only a fool gives soothing sirup to his children when they need surgery.

"None can stay His hand" (Daniel 4).

186.

Man's efforts are indeed futile if he will not hearken to God.

He has no right to complain of the suffering he encounters in the darkness. He need only walk in the Light.

"The Lord will take away from thee all sickness." (Deuteronomy 7.)

187.

God "permits" us to wander from Him.

God *causes* us to suffer if we do so.

Joy is inherent in obedience. It is its reward.

Suffering is inherent in disobedience. "Verily I say unto you, They have *their* reward." (Matthew 6.) (Italics are ours.)

Separation from the Source is the cause of all our ills.

God reaches for man: "Underneath are the ever-lasting arms." (Deuteronomy 23.)

Man "turns and goes his own way": "Adam and his wife hid themselves from the presence of the Lord." (Genesis 3.)

God reaches for man: "The Lord shall be thine everlasting light." (Isaiah 60.)

Man refuses to open the door: "The Light shineth in the darkness; and the darkness comprehended it not." (John 1.)

189.

It is always a cause for sorrow to a Christian that those he loves will not give themselves to God and that he may not see them in the future life.

Many persist in thinking they will be given "another opportunity" in a life hereafter. Is there any basis for such a hope, or is the wish the only authority for the thought?

Why do men and women think they would accept in another life that which they are offered so plainly now?

If they will not hear "Moses and the prophets" they will not "be persuaded, though one rose from the dead." (Luke 16.)

Many are not persuaded although Christ rose from the dead.

190.

"I have withholden the rain from you . . . yet have ye not returned unto me . . .

"I have sent among you the pestilence . . . yet have ye not returned unto me.

"I have overthrown some of you . . . yet have ye not returned unto Me.

"Therefore thus will I do unto thee . . . prepare to meet they God." (Amos 4.)

God's judgments are irrevocable against those who are wilfully and persistently disobedient. He may forbid us to even pray for them. (Jeremiah 14.) (1 John 5.)

191.

We could not be happy in heaven unless we had been prepared for it in this life. The spiritual man's heaven would be hell to the natural man.

Our life here is for our development as spiritual men. When we have been filled with God the only reason for our remaining here is that He can use us to bring others to Him.

The physical death of regenerate man is his reward. Our thinking is all astray if we regard it as a calamity.

Today shalt thou be with Me in Paradise (Luke 23).

"Precious in the sight of the Lord is the death of His saints" (Psalm 116).

PART VIII

192.

When we have committed ourselves and all that we have to God, we can be absolutely certain that He will provide for all our needs.

As natural men, we try to provide for our needs first, and seek God afterwards. Jesus tells us to reverse this order.

"Seek ye first the Kingdom of God and His righteousness; and all these things shall be added unto you." (Matthew 6.)

193.

"What doth the Lord require of thee, but to do justly, and to love mercy, and to walk humbly with thy God." (Micah 6.)

194.

"We know that all things work together for good to them that love God." (Romans 8.)

"Prove me now herewith, said the Lord of hosts, if I will not open you the windows of heaven, and pour you out a blessing that there shall not be room enough to receive it." (Malachi 3.)

"Eye hath not seen, nor ear heard, neither have entered into the heart of man, the things which God hath prepared for them that love Him." (1 Corinthians 2.)

"Lo, I am with you always, even unto the end of the world." (Matthew 28.)

196.

Jesus tells us to "come to" Him, to "follow" Him, and to "abide" in Him.

We can "come to" Jesus and leave Him again if we wish to do so. It is the staying with Him which gives us supernatural power.

It is only when we live with Him—"abide in" Him —that we have the right to expect His fruits and gifts.

All His promises are for those who abide.

Abiding means obedience as to both our characters and activities. It means righteousness and fruit bearing.

197.

If we find that the promises of Jesus are not fulfilled in our lives, we tend to dilute them to conform to our powers. This stops our progress.

Instead of ceasing to expect the fulfillment of His promises, we should inquire: "what is the matter with *me?*"

Even His commands are promises, and if we have difficulties with practical problems we should ask God to show us where we are unclean or unsurrendered.

Until we have been converted from natural men into spiritual men we do not obey even the first commandment. We have an idol in us—our self.

The idol hates the word "surrender." He hates the command that he must die and be born anew.

He has ears, but he pretends not to hear. When asked to surrender often he starts talking about something else.

He is our worst enemy. He prevents the fulfillment of our heart's desire. When God draws nigh, our idol makes "smoke screens" and tries to hide from Him.

When we find "smoke screens" on our lips or in our minds, we must recognize them for what they are. We should laugh at them and blow them away, so that God can destroy the idol and enter into us with His love and gifts.

Trying to convince ourselves that we cannot surrender, or that we have not time for prayer, or that Jesus did not mean His teachings to be taken literally are types of "smoke screens."

The smugness which declares that we are "doing our best" is a "smoke screen." Jesus never asked us to do our best.

The scriptures tell us that our best is "foolishness" and "filthiness" to God. We must be emptied of our worst and our best if we would be filled with the Spirit of God.

When we succeed in living up to our own code of conduct, or that of others about us, our satisfaction with ourselves forms a barrier which makes it difficult for us to receive that which Christ teaches. We cannot accept that which is essential for our salvation if we think we already have it.

"What is the matter with me?" "Am I not all right as I am?" These are the questions of the unimaginative and of the egotist.

201.

Jesus was resurrected because He said "not my will but Thine be done"—because He consented to the crucifixion.

"The law and the prophets were until John: from that time the gospel of the Kingdom of God is preached, and every man entereth violently into it."

We enter into it through the death of the nature with which we are born. "We which live are always delivered unto death for Jesus' sake that the life also of Jesus might be made manifest in our mortal flesh" (2 Corinthians 4).

202.

Any condition which renders man secure without effort on his part causes him to deteriorate.

God works. Christ works.

There is work however which we cannot do.

We cannot convert ourselves or cleanse ourselves.

As to these, we need only do the trusting. God does the work.

We have, "A God . . . which worketh for him that waiteth for Him." (Isaiah 64.)

203.

We did not create ourselves, and we cannot re-create ourselves.

Creation and growth come from God.

The lilies neither "toil nor spin": God causes them to grow.

Trying and straining to grow in grace is useless and exhausting.

If we rely on ourselves and our efforts, we fail and become luke-warm or skeptical.

204.

"No one cometh unto the Father but by Me."

We cannot find the Father excepting through the working of Christ upon us.

We cannot be like the Father—we cannot be united with the Father—excepting through the working of Christ within us.

205.

The new covenant is very different from the old covenant. Man tried to cleanse and sanctify himself, and failed, even with the help of God from the outside. Christ offers to come into us and transform us from the inside.

The Cross of God is not our cross. We cannot

develop a new nature. We must approach our problem *from a different direction*. We must deny our nature and allow the living Christ to enter into us, so that He can give us His nature.

206.

We must not concentrate on righteousness.
We must concentrate on surrender.
We must allow God to make us righteous.

207.

Christianity is not merely an ethical system or moral code. It far transcends these. It is living union with God in Christ.

It is devotion to the Person of Jesus Christ. "Thou shalt love the Lord thy God with all thy heart, and with all thy soul, and with all thy mind."

Jesus Christ, is the Lord, our God.

We must not merely love the man. We must love the Man as God.

208.

If our emotions do not have an outlet, they are liable to back up in us.

Finding God and walking with Him are often very emotional experiences. If we restrain the expression of our feelings upon a high level we may find them working upon a low level.

"Quenching the Spirit" may cause us to revert to that which we were before He entered us.

Spiritual repression (as well as natural frustration) may bring mental impurity.

We prove our love for Jesus when we die with Him
—die to our own nature—and allow Him to enter us
and control us.

We prove our love for Jesus when we allow Him to
make us like Himself by uniting us with God.

We must be sensitive to listen to that which God
wants us to *do*.

Plenty of work is suggested in the Bible!

We cannot do everything.

We must ask the Holy Spirit: "What wilt Thou
have *me* do?" (Italics are ours.)

Work does not always produce good results. It
may produce bad results, if it is in the wrong direction.

We must be careful to ascertain God's will for us
regarding others before we attempt to serve them.

Our work should always originate in Him. Otherwise it may merely satisfy our desire for activity.

It is His wisdom and power—not our energy—that
is effective.

When the Spirit of God enters into us, He changes
our *disposition*. He changes our *desires*.

We hate much that we have loved.

Things which were bitter become sweet. "I delight
to do thy will, O my God."

The only way in which we can do something for God is to do something for our neighbor.

"All the law is fulfilled in one word, even this; Thou shalt love thy neighbor as thyself."

How much do we love ourselves?

What do we do for ourselves?

Do we do this for our neighbor?

214.

God will not strengthen our will; He will not help us in our plans; and He will not help us to be that which we think is good.

He will not patch up our old nature—mend old cloth with new.

He insists upon having a new bottle for His new wine.

215.

The "renewing of our minds," the "having that mind in us which is in Christ," namely our sanctification, is God's work in those who have been born again.

We "die daily" to our old nature only after the birth of Christ's nature in us.

216.

Men use all sorts of stratagems in trying to avoid consenting to the death of self—the old nature.

They become atheists; deny the deity of Christ; attempt to obey the commandments and be "good" by their own power; make regular confession of their sins; and live up to rules of their own formulation, which may or may not be included in the teachings of Christ.

They dedicate their lives to social service; or even become active in religious work, trying to obtain peace, in order to avoid giving control of themselves to the Master.

"None of those men . . . shall taste of my supper." (Luke 14.)

217.

We are born with varying temperaments and ideals.

Some of us go through life very easily—there is not a strong pull in us either upward or downward.

Life is more difficult to others, but through experience they may more readily realize their inadequacy. When they realize they are not sufficient unto themselves they are often vital instruments when they have placed themselves in the hands of God.

PART IX

218.

The Christian life is the easiest way.

Drifting brings us to the rocks.

Walking without God takes us through the swamps and quicksand.

Walking with God is an ascent, but there is a reward for every step which we take with Him.

219.

"The Father abiding in me doeth the work."

We must have faith "in the power that worketh in us."

The Way is by surrender—identification—not by imitation.

When we are identified with Christ, He works in us as God worked in Him.

220.

If we had power in ourselves to be that which we should be, or if it was possible for us to generate power, it would not have been necessary for Jesus to die.

"Forbid it, Lord, that I should boast,
Save in the cross of Christ, my God."

221.

We must *let Christ* clean out the natural antipathies which set up resistance to the power and love which He wants to flow through us.

He will give us both the desire and power to do His will if we wait on Him. "It is God which worketh in you both to will and to do His good pleasure."

If we fight our sins—discipline ourselves—our continuous recognition of their presence makes it more difficult for God to purify and sanctify us. We are sanctified by faith. (Acts 26.)

222.

"There are two ways in which a believer can encounter and strive against sin.

"One is to endeavor to head it off with all his might, seeking his strength in the Word and in prayer. In this form of conflict we use the power of the will.

"The other is to turn at the very moment of the temptation to the Lord Jesus in the silent exercise of faith and say to Him: 'Lord I have no strength. Thou art my keeper.' This is the method of faith. This is the victory that overcometh the world, even your faith." (Murray.)

223.

The troubles of some of us come from trying to imitate Jesus. We use self-discipline and self-effort under various disguises.

If we are persistent we may be brought to hair shirts and lonely cells!

Many a monk had no time for evangelism because he was too busy trying to purify himself.

Gallantry and stoicism are not The Way.

224.

Under the old covenant, men sought to keep the commandments and failed.

Under the new covenant, God offers to send His Holy Spirit to live His life in us. The commandments are promises which He will fulfill in us.

Our initial humility in confessing our sinfulness and inadequacy must be followed by a deeper one. We must know that we can never be anything else as of ourselves.

He must be and do *all*. We must lose *all* confidence in the flesh.

225.

We have not attained real humility if we say: "I am not worthy yet." We never can be worthy.

We must surrender our unworthiness to God. This means the surrender of all self-reliance and self-effort as to our sanctification. It means accepting His cleansing power by faith. It must be all grace.

226.

God performs both sides of the new covenant *regarding our sanctification* if we let Him enter us and fill us and do not try to perform any part ourselves. We become "workers with Him" when we allow Him to will and to do.

We are blameless if our surrender is complete. Our faith is "counted as righteousness" because it receives Him who is our righteousness.

At first, we are considered righteous because of our faith.

Later, we are righteous because our faith has enabled Him to make use righteous.

It is God who will "Make you perfect in every good work to do His will, working in you that which is well pleasing in His sight, through Jesus Christ." (Hebrews 13.)

227.

When His Spirit has entered us and has filled us we no longer need rules. When we live in the Light we do not need lanterns to guide us.

When we love God and our neighbor we do not have to even think of the law.

"If righteousness come by the law, then Christ is dead in vain.

"The law was our schoolmaster to bring us unto Christ.

"The life which I now live . . . I live by the faith of the Son of God." (Galatians 2 and 3.)

"What then? shall we sin, because we are not under the law? . . . God forbid. Know ye not, that to whom ye yield yourselves . . . His servants ye are to . . . obey." (Romans 6.)

When we ask men, women and children merely to live up to a code of ethics we are asking them to live "under the law"—under the old covenant.

When we ask them to accept Christ as their Master we can know that if they do so, that He will cause them to be "dead to the law," that is, He will change their *desires,* and make them *want* to live up to His code, and will give them the power.

In one case we are asking them to do that which may make them resentful and unhappy. We are asking them to do that which is impossible for them in their own power.

In the other case we are asking them to do that which God makes possible, and which will fill them with joy.

To be "dead to sin" means that we *need* not sin. To be "dead to the law" means we have *no inclination* to break the law.

Love fulfills the law.

The world is full of old covenant teachers who are telling us, in Sunday Schools and in colleges, that as unregenerate men we can be good if we really "try." They are teaching that our higher nature can cast out our lower nature: that self can overcome or lift self.

To God, "there is no difference" between our higher and lower nature. He knows that selfishness and un-truth are interwoven all through us.

We need new covenant teachers to tell us that we will always be what God considers evil unless we let His Holy Spirit come into us and make us righteous —unless we let Him be our righteousness.

230.

Our part consists in working out that which God enables us to will and do. We must co-operate with Him.

He will carry us if we are unable to walk, but we must not expect to be carried if He has given us the power to walk.

If our arm is paralyzed we cannot stretch forth our hand, but if He cures us we must not expect Him to raise it for us.

We must *believe* and *act*.

First: I can do nothing as of myself.

Second: I can do all things through Christ within me.

231.

Our difficulty often is in knowing when we are working in the wisdom and power of God, and when we are using the wisdom and power of man.

If we go to God in prayer and ask Him to search our hearts, He will disclose to us any vestiges of self-reliance.

When we eliminate these we are thrown back upon faith in God.

"Every Christian renounces this nominally, but the habit of self-reliance has so incorporated itself with his being . . . that he does not easily discover how much he is under the influence of it." (Bowen.)

God expects us to do much more than that which is usually meant when we speak of His will.

He expects us, not only to follow His commandments, but also to consult Him as to our career. We must not do our planning and ask His help. We must allow Him to lead us where He will.

"A true walk with God will do more to awaken awe, wonder and amazement in your soul than would a century of travel through the sights of earth . . . Tear into small pieces any itinerary for the journey which your imagination may have drawn up." ("The Life of Faith"—London.)

233.

The humility to be willing to obey God is the gate through which we must pass before we can know Him and be born again.

Increasing faith comes because of our experiences with Him.

Faith is the antidote to fear.

Fear vanishes when we have a true humility, and know that God loves us.

234.

When we *know* that we are nothing excepting as from God, we realize that we have nothing to lose as of ourselves. Confident in His love, we hold ourselves ready to receive His gifts.

"Without Thee I am dust: only because of Thee am I a living soul and a quickened spirit born into Thy Kingdom."

God's "strength is made perfect in weakness." (2 Corinthians 12.) He can use us when we are humble and allow His power to flow through us: when we are so "weak" that we do not resist His will.

235.

St. Paul warns us against complicating the simplicity of the Gospel.

The Gospel is:

If we let Him, Christ Himself will enter us and make us like Himself.

We need only trust and obey Him.

If we are willing to obey, Christ will enable us to walk with Him.

Our troubles come because of our pride—we want to walk in our own power. They come because we are so stubborn as to resist Him consciously or unconsciously.

If we do not trust Him, He must bring us to a place where we are compelled to do so if we are to be saved.

236.

If we rely partially on God and partially upon ourselves, we are liable to fall between the spiritual and the natural.

In the nature of things it is necessary that we rely *solely* on God. If we are not willing to do so, we do best when we concentrate upon the powers He has given us as natural men.

When we make a partial surrender we have two wills in us: we are a "divided personality." We are kept very "busy" if we try to do the will of God and that which we think we ought to do.

When we make a complete surrender and are filled with the Spirit, we are a different person than we were before our conversion. We are "new creatures."

Instead of our old mind, we have Christ's mind in us. Instead of our will, we are controlled by God's will. We seek to have *no will of our own:* "not my will, but Thine."

Many of us would be very content to have even the memory of the old man completely blotted out.

238.

Saul was the natural man. *Paul* was the spiritual man, born of God. "St. Paul" was the God-filled man.

Paul was the regenerated spirit. "St. Paul" was the Spirit of God in the regenerated spirit.

"It is no longer I (Paul) but Christ who liveth in me."

239.

We have as much of the Holy Spirit as we have faith.

We increase our faith through understanding the promises of Jesus and by experiencing their fulfillment in us.

We increase our faith by increasing the area of our surrender.

When we have surrendered all, and the Holy Spirit has cleansed us from sin, we have "confidence toward God," and "we know that we have the petitions which we have asked of Him."

240.

When we stumble, we should go directly to God, ask forgiveness, and press forward.

Nothing is gained by whining about our unworthiness. We never can be worthy as of ourselves.

"He said unto me, Son of man, stand upon thy feet and I will speak unto thee." (Ezekiel 2.)

"Gird up thy loins now like a man." (Job 40.)

241.

We must "put away childish things."

Boastfulness, or desire to be "prominent," is always childish and may come from an "inferiority complex."

Immorality often comes from vanity.

Vanity is sometimes superficial and harmless to others.

We can know that conceit is deeply rooted in us when we judge others by the standard of that which we are ourselves; or when we disbelieve in that which others claim to have because we have not attained it.

242.

We cannot make any progress in the spiritual life if we do not forgive everyone.

"If ye forgive men their trespasses your heavenly

Father will also forgive you. But if ye forgive not men their trespasses neither will your Father forgive your trespasses." (Matthew 6.)

"Forgive if ye have aught against anyone; that your Father also which is in heaven may forgive your trespasses." (Mark 11.)

"If thou bring thy gift to the altar, and there rememberest that thy brother hath aught against thee;

"Leave there thy gift before the altar, and go thy way; first be reconciled to thy brother, and then come and offer thy gift." (Matthew 5.)

243.

When we are filled with the Spirit of God there is never any question of "doing our duty." We *are* good Samaritans. When we are filled with God, we are filled with Love.

"I was an hungered, and ye gave me meat: I was thirsty and ye gave me drink: I was a stranger and ye took me in: naked, and ye clothed me: I was in prison and ye came unto me.

"Inasmuch as ye did it unto one of these my brethren, even these least, ye did it unto me." (Matthew 25.)

244.

"Mary . . . sat at the Lord's feet, and heard his word.

But Martha was cumbered about much serving." (Luke 10.)

Mary was receiving understanding and supernatural power.

If we try to serve the Lord or others with our own power we become anxious and troubled.

If we drink of Him, we become wells of living water to quench the thirst of many.

"Mary hath chosen the good part, which shall not be taken away from her."

245.

"It is not reason that *we* should leave the word of God, and serve tables . . . But *we* will give ourselves continually to prayer, and to the ministry of the word." (Acts 6.) (Italics are ours.)

Some one must serve tables. It was the will of God that Brother Laurence spend his life cooking in a monastery. We must never care whether our part is to be seemingly great or small.

"Lord what wilt Thou have *me* do." (Italics are ours.)

PART X.

246.

Prayer must be an ascent of the soul to the Source.

247.

Prayer is a striving to find our way "through the veil" to an identification with God.

248.

Speaking generally, through prayer we travel from our state as natural men to union with God by a series of crises and processes.

249.

There are two great landmarks in the Christian life: our rebirth, and our being *filled* with the Spirit.

Until we are born anew, God works upon us from the outside.

When we *believe*, His Holy Spirit enters our spirit and works from the inside.

Thereafter "His Spirit beareth witness with our spirit that we are the children of God."

If God's Spirit does not enter us it is because our belief is only an intellectual one.

250.

At regeneration it may seem to us that "our" forces are being released.

A clearer vision enables us to understand that we are born anew through a combination of forces without us and of potential forces within us.

Dormant forces within us are released by the instreaming of Life—the Holy Spirit—from the outside.

Our powers are dependent upon the continuing influx of that new Life.

251.

The philosophy that we are but as grains of sand and can do nothing to influence events is a deadly one.

Jesus tells us that which we can do. He tells us to enlist in His Kingdom and recruit others.

He tells us that if we are united with Him that He will use us to change the course of events. St. Paul and Wesley changed history.

252.

A man does not progress according to his powers as much as according to his wants. If he is self-satisfied, he drifts downward.

If man realizes his inadequacy he is on the road to greater things.

"God, change my desires. Help me to want to be like Thee, as manifested in Jesus."

Why are not more people seeking God?

We find the main reason for this in Genesis: like Adam, they do not think they need Him.

They are not seeking Him because of their stupidity, and their appalling conceit.

They are not seeking Him because of their lack of imagination. They do not realize all that which may befall them without Him. They do not realize all that He is offering them.

254.

We turn to God when there is a conjunction of two conditions:

When we realize our inadequacy and realize that God is offering us an opportunity.

Stated differently, we turn to God:

When we feel a need, and understand that God will fulfill it.

When we are convicted of sin and its power, and realize that Christ saves and gives us His power.

When we realize we have no source of power in ourselves, but learn that God, the Source, can be drawn upon.

255.

It is a God-given "change of heart" and "difference in our mental attitude" which spells success or failure in the spiritual life. "Rend your heart and not your garments." (Joel 2.)

"Your sins have withholden good things from you

. . . Ask for the old paths, where there is the good way, and walk therein." (Jeremiah 5-6.)

256.

We can be sure God's will is going to be done; that "His plans will be brought to pass."

Our choice is as to whether we will walk joyously with Him or whether we will use our freedom to resist Him.

Resistance to God always means mental or physical suffering.

"I kill, and I make alive; I wound, and I heal: neither is there any that can deliver out of my hand." (Deuteronomy 32.)

257.

If we obey: "I will put none of these diseases upon thee." (Exodus 15.) "Be not afraid, neither be thou dismayed." "I will not fail thee nor forsake thee." (John 1.)

If we disobey: "I will smite them with the pestilence." (Numbers 14.) "The Lord shall smite thee with madness and blindness." (Deuteronomy 28.)

"As a man chasteneth his son, so the Lord thy God chasteneth thee."

"Whom the Lord loveth He chasteneth . . . for our profit that we might be partakers of His Holiness." (Hebrews 12.)

258.

If we are satisfied with ourselves and our lives, we may not have any conscious desire to find God.

Many of us do not believe it is possible to find Him

in spite of the testimony of millions who have found Him.

Many of us want to find God, but do not know how to find Him. We feel that there must be conditions for us to comply with, but we do not meet a teacher or interpreter who can explain them to us.

No one can show us The Way who has not taken it himself. We cannot give to others that which we do not possess.

"I am against the prophets, saith the Lord, that steal my words every one from his neighbor." (Jeremiah 23.)

259.

We need not talk much about sin. We need only bring men and women to Christ. If we try to convict them of sin, they are liable to run away from God and from us.

Our duty is to acquaint them with our Saviour and Master—to tell them what He has done and is doing for us. The conviction of sin is the work of the Holy Spirit.

260.

"Our holiness does not consist in our changing and becoming better ourselves: it is rather *He*, He Himself, born and growing in us, in such a way as to fill our hearts, and to drive out our natural self, "our old man," which cannot itself improve, and whose destiny is only to perish . . .

"The distinction between the preparatory operation of the Spirit *upon* man, by means of external manifestation, and His actual dwelling *in* man seems almost effaced from Christian consciousness." (Godet.)

261.

We often talk of "receiving Christ," of "self-surrender," of "giving God possession" as though He was only outside of us. In this case, we continue to fight our own battles asking His help. Instead of doing this, we must realize our inadequacy to bear the brunt of the battle ourselves, and must let the Christ *within* fight the battle for us.

262.

"For how long a period even after the Reformation were the doctrines of the Holy Ghost . . . and His indwelling in the believer, almost unknown." (Saphir.)

"The indwelling Spirit has indeed been given to every child of God . . . We have the Holy Spirit within us; only he who is faithful in the lesser will receive the greater . . .

"If we would only believe that Christ, the Jehovah God, our Creator actually abides in us, how He would make our life the proof of His Almighty power!" (Murray.)

263.

We find our way "through the veil" to the Living Christ by the adventure of abandoning ourselves to Him. When we do so, He comes "through the veil," and enters us, *living His Life in us*.

We are anxious to forget that the "old" man ever

existed. We hope that even the "new" man will be unnoticed and unknown so that the glory of Christ can flow through us.

We are anxious to be hid in the Vine, giving glory to the Vine for all the fruit.

264.

The Holy Spirit is the "indwelling Christ." "Know ye not your own selves, how that Jesus Christ is *in you*." This is the "mystery which has been hid from ages and generations, but now is made manifest to His saints . . . which is Christ *in you* the hope of glory." (Italics are ours.)

265.

It is important that we should realize that He has entered us.

We would not have been born again if He had not entered us.

The Holy Spirit is the Spirit of Adoption and we are not children of God until He has entered us and regenerated our spirit. "If any man have not the Spirit of Christ, he is none of His."

It is easier for us to realize "the promise of the Father"—"that ye might be filled with all the fulness of God"—if we know that Christ is within us.

266.

We must not only "believe." We must *receive*.

We cannot be said to have received Him unless His indwelling presence has *reached our consciousness*.

A man may be cured of a disease, but unless he knows it, his restored life has no value to him. Many men have been cured of illness but have remained seemingly ill because they were unconvinced as to having been healed. They were *really* cured, but were not *actually* well.

If we do not know that Christ has entered us, we cannot *experience* the newness of life which has been given us. It is important "that Christ may dwell in your hearts by faith."

267.

Unless we know that Christ—His Holy Spirit—is within us, cleansing and sanctifying us, we are liable to attempt these things ourselves.

He is our righteousness, sanctification and redemption. He will increase if we are willing to decrease. If we offer no resistance—if we are "meek" or "weak" —He becomes strong in us.

When we are reborn the Kingdom of Heaven is within us. We have as much of God as we have faith.

"The Kingdom of heaven is like unto leaven, which a woman took, and hid in three measures of meal, till the whole is leavened." If we believe, it permeates, purifies and fills us.

Christ, Himself, permeates, purifies and fills us.

PART XI.

268.

If we go to God, humble enough to be teachable, and desire the truth *whatever it may be,* we can always be sure we will find it.

We need only pray to the GOD WHO IS. He will lead us to Christ. "Everyone that hath heard from the Father, and hath learned, cometh unto me."

269.

The only reason we have to wait upon God is because He knows we are not ready.

He is eager to bestow all now. Our searching for God is really God reaching for us. Our waiting upon Him is His waiting for us.

Are we ready to comply with all the conditions?

Are we prepared to have the disapproval and even dislike of everyone we know, excepting God?

"If the world hate you, ye know that it hated me before it hated you." (John 15.)

270.

It is impossible for natural man to understand God, or to understand other spiritual men.

Jesus was accused of being "beside Himself." (Mark 3.)

The apostles were accused of being drunk. (Acts 2.)

Festus said to St. Paul: "thou art beside thyself; much learning doth make thee mad." (Acts 26.)

271.

Jesus told Peter that only God could reveal to him that He is the Christ, the Son of the living God. St. Paul tells us "No man can say that Jesus is the Lord but by the Holy Ghost."

If we have received a revelation from God we have no right to become arrogant, or angry with those who have not. We have no justification for any feeling of superiority.

We did not find God because of our goodness or our intelligence. It is more likely that we found Him in the Valley of Humiliation.

272.

When we are born anew we *begin* our spiritual life. We are no longer merely natural men: we are what St. Paul calls "babes in Christ."

We must continue to rely on God. He cleanses and keeps on cleansing. Self cannot cast out self: Satan cannot cast out Satan.

Our mind is renewed, as the leaven of the Spirit of God works in us. We are cleansed mystically by the blood of Christ.

We wait on God until we are ready to be filled with His Spirit.

At Pentecost the disciples were *filled with the Spirit*. This is the "enduement of power from on high"—the "pearl of great price."

It is the gift of the Holy Spirit—of Christ, Himself —in His Fulness.

The "new bottle" is *filled* with new wine.

When we know we cannot as of ourselves make our ideals real, God gives us the power to do so if we let Him.

When we enlist, God guides.

When we are receptive, God enters us.

When we are willing and ready to be filled, God fills us with Himself.

We receive the fulness of God when we are so emptied of self that His possession of us makes us no longer "I," but Christ living His life in us.

From God's side, He gives Himself, and continues to do so. He gives Himself and all He is. We must *receive*—must "believe that we have received."

He is not *"given in measure."* Our mistake is in trying to *receive* only a part of Him.

We receive Him by faith; He dwells in us by faith; we are sanctified by faith; we are filled with Him by faith.

The being filled with the Holy Spirit is as definite an act of God, as is our rebirth. Like our rebirth, it may take place slowly or suddenly.

It is when we know of the invincible power of sin in us as natural men, that we pray for the full power of Christ.

After we have "appropriated" the promise we will have to wait for the manifestation if our surrender is not complete. No amount of "claiming" will take the place of absolute committal of self. We must be self-emptied to be Christ-filled.

277.

Before Pentecost, the apostles

1. Continued in prayer and supplication.

2. They were "with one accord"—united.

3. They were joyful because they believed the promises of Jesus.

4. They were persistent. They prayed and waited "until" they received the outward manifestation.

278.

"It is in the union and fellowship of believers that the Spirit can manifest His full power. It was to the hundred and twenty continuing in one place together, and praying with one accord, that the Spirit came from the throne of the glorified Lord." (Murray.)

279.

Christ was only an external Christ to the apostles while He was with them. "Ye know Him; for He dwelleth *with* you, and *shall be in* you." In spite of their contact with Him, and in spite of His teachings, they leaned upon Him—upon the Man.

At Pentecost He not only came and *dwelt in them* but also *filled* them. "Rivers of living water" overflowed from them to others. There was not "room in them to receive" Him.

280.

Sins which we cannot see may make it necessary for us to "tarry"—to "quietly wait on the Lord."

We do not have to wait for the Spirit for the reason the apostles had to "tarry" (because He was "not yet"). Christ *is* risen. He *is* glorified.

We are willing to share His glory. Are we willing first to share His afflictions?

281.

St. Paul was reborn on the road to Damascus, and was filled with the Spirit three days later.

Many have not been filled with the Spirit until years after their new birth. They have not complied with the conditions: they have not completely given themselves to Christ.

282.

The fulness of the Spirit comes as a result of prayer.

It comes as a result of faith.

It comes as a result of perfect surrender.

We are continuously filled if we continuously surrender all. If we abide in the Vine the sap always flows through us.

283.

When we hate our life *as natural men* and want to lose *that life,* we are prepared to receive the full, overflowing life of God.

284.

Worldly genius is the breaking through of the limitations of natural man. It is often fragmentary and one-sided. It is possessing and being possessed by "something" outside of oneself.

The Spirit-filled man has open to him all "the treasures of wisdom and knowledge."

285.

When we are willing to belong to God and to serve our fellow men, and are filled with His Spirit, we are prepared to do His work. We use supernatural power under His authority and direction.

Stated more accurately, He uses us.

286.

There is a vast difference between working for God, and allowing God to work through us. God can use us fully only when we come to Him empty-handed.

Our worldly experiences are only because of His permissive will. They are not part of His order. He allows them so that we will be convinced of our inadequacy.

God does not want gifts. He wants us. He wants to exercise *His* wisdom, power and love through us.

We must be willing to abandon all of our assets if we would have the pearl of great price.

It is often when we surrender the qualifications which we value most that He is able to live His life in us.

"Nothing in my hand I bring,
  Simply to Thy Cross I cling."

The wire to God is always open. We sometimes have *difficulty* in listening to Him, because our memory, worldly pictures, "powers of the air," and "rulers of the darkness" are interfering with our reception of Him (Ephesians 6). But nothing outside of ourselves "shall be able to *separate* us from the love of God, which is in Jesus Christ our Lord." (Romans 8.)

PART XII.

288.

The Bible can be understood by us only as it is interpreted for us by the Holy Spirit.

Only the Living Word can know the meaning of the Written Word.

289.

God is the only ultimate fact.

We can have Christ-consciousness when He is within us.

When He has possession of us, we are wells—not cisterns. We can do and know "all things."

290.

We must realize the actual incarnation of God in us.

We must get ourselves out of the way and let Him function.

When we hate our nature and let it die, we "bringeth forth much fruit" (John 12).

291.

We sometimes keep on asking God for powers which are already in us.

If we have admitted Christ, we *have* His power, understanding and love.

We have *Him*.

292.

We are apt to think of truth as an idea, proposition or abstraction.

Jesus Christ was so filled with truth and life that He said "I am the way, the truth and the life."

In this sense, Love, Truth and the Word are merely different names for Christ.

Mystically, Love—Truth—The Word—is a Person.

293.

As Life and Truth are a Person, we must eat and drink of a Person in order to live and to understand.

Through the mystical drinking of Christ's blood and eating of His flesh, we acquire new Life—new minds and hearts.

"As the living Father hath sent me, and I live by the Father: so he that eateth me, even he shall live by me." (John 6.)

"Take eat; this is my body."

"This is my blood." "Drink all ye of it."

294.

God wants us to be a part of Him—a branch of the Vine.

There are those who would like to have His power and wisdom, and allow Him to keep His goodness—*righteousness*—for Himself.

We cannot take a part of God.

We ask for qualities. God insists upon giving us Himself.

Our fruits are manifestations of His indwelling.

295.

We are a part of Love, Life and Truth when God possesses us.

Our fruits are fortitude, gentleness, goodness, faithfulness, meekness, temperance, peace and joy.

Our fruits are His characteristics.

296.

Spiritual fruits cannot come from natural man. They are the result of spiritual life.

If Life is there, the fruit will be there even if we are unconscious of it.

297.

Christ endured the Cross "for the joy set before Him." (Hebrews 12.)

Our joy on earth consists of:

1. Our knowledge of forgiven sins.

2. Our power over sin.

3. Our being used to save others.

4. Our being in God Himself: "He in us and we in Him."

298.

When we are filled with God, we have no fears. We are secure.

Our desires are changed.

We have power over the nature with which we are born. We have a new heredity.

We have Someone to share our burdens.

We lose our tenseness and restlessness.

We are freed from the slavery of our emotions.

We gain a fresh intellectual clarity.

We sing for joy of heart. The solemn people are those who are still searching.

299.

When we are *filled with Christ* we are living *in Christ*. Our life is "hid with Christ in God."

We are serene. On the one hand, we do not take responsibilities which do not belong to us: "the government of the world is on His shoulder."

On the other hand, we are alert to do all He asks us to do by His Word and His Holy Spirit.

When our feet are planted firmly on The Rock, we are qualified to help others out of the pit and show them The Way.

When we do this we know what is meant by sharing in His joy.

300.

When we are filled with God we are filled with Love.

Love is patient, kind, generous, humble, courteous, unselfish, good tempered, guileless, sincere, and pure.

If there is anyone we do not love, we can know that it is still the old "I" which has control of us. We are not yet "crucified with Christ."

301.

Nothing could be more definite than the Biblical promises regarding guidance.

"He will guide you even unto death."

"Trust in the Lord with all thine heart; and lean not unto thine own understanding. In all thy ways acknowledge Him, and He shall direct thy paths."

"Commit thy works unto the Lord, and thy thoughts shall be established."

"The Comforter which is the Holy Ghost, whom the Father will send in my name, he shall teach you all things."

"When he, the Spirit of truth is come, he will guide you into all truth."

"The anointing which ye have received of Him abideth in you, and ye need not that any man shall teach you."

302.

"If ye abide in me, and my words abide in you, ask whatsoever ye will, and it shall be done unto you." (John 15.) (Italics are ours.)

If we are not abiding in Him, that is, if we have not given ourselves to Him, and are not blameless in His sight, our prayers may not be answered and we cannot expect divine guidance.

"If ye keep my commandments, ye shall abide in my love." (John 15.)

303.

We hear it said that we should "check our guidance by common sense." This is applicable to those who are not abiding.

They must check the thoughts coming to them by reason and experience. Their thoughts may be only "hunches."

It has no application to those who are filled with the Spirit. They know how to "test the Spirits." They know His Voice.

304.

Spiritual understanding comes through obedience. "Let him become a fool that he may be wise."

Rationalism is the highest attribute of natural man.

God's guidance is for the man who has been born from above.

God does not ask us to throw away our mind. He asks us to give it up to Him.

He knows all the facts.

If we surrender our reasoning to Him because it is not good enough, He will *establish our thoughts*.

If we insist upon leaning upon our own understanding, He cannot direct our paths.

The meek will He guide in judgment (Psalm 25).

305.

When a man says that "sound sense and sound religion always go together," we suppose he means *his* "sound sense." What about the "sound sense" of Smith, Jones and Brown?

The enthronement of reason is always anti-Christ.

Jesus taught that which seems irrational to natural and carnal man. "Ye know not the scriptures, nor the power of God." (Mark 12.)

Such knowledge as man can gain of himself—now called scholarship—is his great temptation.

306.

When we are reborn and are willing to be *led blindly* by God, He will let us know, when ideas come to us, whether they are from Him or not from Him. If we are not sure, we need only "wait on Him," and He will lead us through all confusion.

Jesus Christ did not tell us to trust common sense. The Sermon on the Mount is not common sense. It is above common sense. He told us to trust His Word and the guidance of His Holy Spirit.

God does not tell us to use our faculties. He tells us to present them to Him as a living sacrifice, so that He can use them.

307.

There is a clear cut line between mental science and Christianity; between the science of psychology and spiritual power; between the life of reason and the spiritual life; and between common sense and faith.

God gives us the freedom to choose between them. The "old" man glorifies his reason and experience. The "new" man, because of his surrender and experience with God, has faith.

Man never rises so high as when he does not know where he is going, provided he is following God's command.

308.

To be a "fool for Christ" does not mean that man should act upon all ideas or impulses coming to him.

It means that the reborn should acknowledge that God knows all the facts, and that man does not; and that therefore man's wisdom is as foolishness to God.

It means he should realize that he must take time to listen to such directions, as to his character and activities, as God may send him through His Holy Spirit. It means that he should have the humility and the courage to act on such directions.

309.

There may not be any supernatural power in the water of the Jordan, or in the brazen serpent; but there is supernatural power in obedience—in faith.

We obtain knowledge by exercising our intellectual curiosity. We obtain wisdom and power through obedience.

Wider circles of understanding and faith come to us when we do things *because God tells us to do them*.

310.

It is difficult to leave our problems surrendered with God. We tend to make a mental surrender and then assume the burden again.

We must let Him take all *responsibility*. This does not necessarily mean that we are to forget our problems. We must listen to Him as to whether there is anything He wants us to do about them. We must watch Him solve them or wait for guidance as to the part which He assigns us.

It is a tragic mistake to try to convince ourselves that we are relying on God in any department of our lives if we have not the faith to do so.

We can know that if there are any doubts or fears in our minds or hearts, that we have not given Him complete possession of us.

If we abandon our own reason, and have not sufficient faith, we may find ourselves completely helpless.

It is a mistake to think that "God does not want to be bothered with trifles."

He wants us to keep in touch with Him every moment—to "pray without ceasing." It may be important that we should be kept poor or ill solely because it will teach us to look to Him constantly.

Any vestige of self-reliance acts as a resistant to His power. We must continuously remain as a branch of the Vine.

The humility to depend on the Life-giving sap without interruption is the quality that enables us to bear fruit.

Worry or sadness will not exist where there is perfect faith.

If we trust completely in God's plan for the world and for us, and "if our heart condemn us not," then we have confidence that "all things work together for good."

If we know that we are doing God's will in every department of our lives, we share His joy. We know that our petitions will be answered.

314.

"Have faith in God. Verily I say unto you, whosoever shall not doubt in his heart, but shall believe that what he saith cometh to pass: he shall have it. Therefore I say unto you, All things whatsoever ye pray and ask for, believe that ye have received them, and ye shall have them." (Mark 11.)

315.

"The earth bringeth forth fruit of herself."

Similarly the Holy Spirit bringeth forth fruit of Himself.

Jesus unfolded Himself as God.

St. Paul *became* filled with God.

Christ reproduces Himself in us if we let Him do it.

PART XIII.

316.

"These signs shall follow them that believe (believe, trust and obey); In my name shall they cast out devils; and they shall speak with new tongues (this is not to be confused with the *gift* of tongues);

"They shall take up serpents; and if they drink any deadly thing, it shall not hurt them; they shall lay hands on the sick, and they shall recover." (Mark 16.)

A "believer" is not one who merely accepts the fact that Jesus is the Son of God. He is one who *believes in Him* enough to deny himself, take up his cross, and follow Him.

317.

The *fruits* of the Spirit develop as we abide in the Vine.

We should "covet the best *gifts*" and pray for them.

They are given to us for the purpose of bringing others into the Kingdom. (1 Peter 4.)

Our natural gifts tend to glorify ourselves. Spiritual gifts glorify God.

St. Paul tells us that prophecy is the greatest of gifts. Under the new covenant this means the power of inspired speaking or writing rather than that of foretelling events.

We are prophets when we are authorized by God to speak for Him.

To some are given "the word of wisdom" (revelation of truth—intuitively).

To some are given "the word of knowledge" (intellectual understanding).

To some are given special faith, or the power to heal, or to work miracles.

To some are given the power to discern spirits, the ability to speak in tongues, or to interpret them. (1 Corinthians 12 and 14.)

When gifts are not received from God it may be because they are not wanted or expected. Our desires or our faith may not be what they should be.

Our *fruits*—that which we *are*—may operate spontaneously.

We must "stir up the *gift* that is in thee." (2 Timothy 1.)

We must *work out* that which God *works in*.

"The spirits of the prophet are subject to the prophets." (1 Corinthians 14.)

Miracles cause people to "take heed" (Acts 8). They *arrest* and *stir*.

The Holy Spirit preaching through us *moves*.

The Holy Spirit teaching through us instructs.

The Church needs all gifts. It needs some to plant and some to water.

We are told to pray for additional gifts and to pray earnestly for the best gifts.

"Ye have not because ye ask not." (James 4.)

323.

Our fruits are manifestations of the life of the indwelling Christ.

Our gifts are manifestations of His power. We cannot, as of ourselves, generate a "passion for souls." When Christ possesses us, He brings souls to Himself.

We speak "not in words which man's wisdom teacheth, but which the Holy Ghost teacheth." (1 Corinthians 2.)

324.

God may give us various powers at any time, and He may withdraw them at any time.

He sometimes uses us when we are unconscious of His doing so.

We have no right to *expect* His gifts unless we have given Him possession of us. *All* His promises are to those who are *abiding in Him*.

Paul and Peter had all or many the gifts of the Spirit because they were God-possessed.

There is the same difference between the mere scholastic theologian and the fruitbearer, as there is between the musician and the musical genius. The first may pass a good examination, but he cannot move others as does the one who has the Spirit.

Our own experiences must always be checked with the Word of God as interpreted by the Holy Spirit.

They must also be checked with the experiences of the Church of Christ—the experiences of those to whom God has revealed Himself.

If we repent and really *believe in* the Lord Jesus Christ—really trust Him completely with our lives, and realize that He has possession of us,—our faulty doctrines—misinterpretation of portions of the scripture—may not interfere with our own peace and joy.

It is essential, however, if we are to teach others, that our theology as to the essentials should be sound. If we do not understand how our own salvation was effected, we may lead others astray by teaching them that which was only incidental to our salvation, or which was necessary for us merely because of our peculiar situation or temperament.

In our search for Truth, none of us need accept that which is told us by others.

We can go direct to God in prayer and ask Him to show us the way to Himself.

If we want Him more than we want all else we will find Him.

Most of us do not want Him more than anything else until we have been through the Valley of Humiliation.

"God, humiliate me before all the world if it will make me realize I am but clay in Thy hands."

329.

Ignorance and stupidity are often the basic causes of our ills. They are often the cause of our disobedience.

It is through them that man may lose his opportunity for the Garden of Eden.

Disobedience—sin—is the great stupidity.

It was because of ignorance, stupidity and disobedience that our Lord was crucified.

"God forgive them for they know not what they do."

330.

"Wisdom is the principal thing; therefore get wisdom: and with all thy getting get understanding." (Proverbs 4.)

"Give me understanding and I shall live." (Psalm 119.)

"Ye have heard Him, and been taught by Him, as the truth is in Jesus" (Ephesians 4), and He is "within you."

Some of us "hate to be wrong."

This is a characteristic which makes it difficult for us to make a full surrender. We instinctively feel that we will find our thinking wrong in many ways when we attain spiritual discernment. In unregenerate man: "All is vanity!"

331.

We must *understand* because if we do not, the seed may be taken from us, even if it is "planted in our hearts."

We must know the truth. We must have the Spirit of truth. We must have Christ.

332.

We must do more than know the truth. We must *be* the embodiment of truth. The Spirit of truth must be in us.

We must more than understand humility, love, purity and faith. We must be humble and pure. We must have faith. We must love.

Understanding will merely make us miserable if we do not act upon it.

333.

St. Paul was called by Jesus Christ to be a witness and an interpreter for Him.

There is no difference between their teachings to those who have been born into spiritual understanding. "To be in Christ" *is* to have eternal life.

If we have been born from above, the Holy Spirit will reconcile words and events that may seem contradictory to us.

We are drawn to God either through our head or our heart.

Both truth and love affect our will.

When love and understanding are joined in us, we have the basis for the faith which unfalteringly follows Jesus.

No amount of knowledge will take the place of personal consecration and personal righteousness.

In fact "the Holy Spirit can only *enlighten* us as He sanctifies us." (Murray.)

"None of the wicked shall understand." (Daniel 12.)

God is waiting to reveal many wonders to us, but He can do so only as we develop spiritually.

Natural man tends to use his power for his own destruction.

The poor will always be with us as long as men are lazy and sensual.

Many are rich because of hard work and self-denial.

The parasite who has lived on the toil of others has no reason for feeling proud.

We sometimes think that God wants the rich to give to the poor in order to help Him make an equal dis-

tribution of goods. God would not want an equal
distribution of goods among carnal men. Many would
be ruined if they were allowed to abound.

Besides, such views assume that the supply of goods
is limited.

God can increase the wealth of the world whenever
He chooses.

We must give to the poor *under His direction*.

339.

All we can do is to plant the seed in good ground.
It does not do any good if we plant it upon rocky
places or among thorns.

"For this people's heart is waxed gross and their
ears are dull of hearing." (Matthew 13.)

"Blessed are your eyes for they see; and your ears
for they hear."

"He that received seed unto the good ground is he
that heareth the word and understandeth it." (Matthew 13.)

340.

We can only tell the story of Jesus and His love.

It is His Holy Spirit who does the work.

We cannot change people. They cannot change
themselves. We must efface ourselves and let the love
of God change them.

341.

To natural man, it seems unfair that men should be
able to live a life of sin, and be forgiven at the eleventh

hour. This reasoning is foolishness to God. It does not comprehend the nature of God, or realize the suffering that is inherent in darkness.

The man who sins until he is old has already paid a part of the penalty. He has "had his reward." He has lived in fear, greed and lust. He has not known love, peace and joy.

342.

Our greatest happiness as carnal man—far above any pleasure of the senses or intellect—is when we have moments of adoration for another. They are unearthly and give us glimpses of the Kingdom of heaven.

We cannot love God until we meet Him. Love and worship come through our experiences with Him, and through our understanding of Him.

When we see ourselves as we are, and get a vision of His holiness, we begin to worship Him.

God knows we are not as we should be if we do not *desire* to worship Him.

343.

"After that ye have suffered a while, (God will) make you perfect, establish, strengthen, settle you." (1 Peter 5.)

"Be ye therefore perfect even as your Father which is in heaven is perfect." (Matthew 5.)

"Be ye holy; for I am holy." (1 Peter 1.)

"That ye may be blameless and harmless, the sons of God, without rebuke, in the midst of a crooked and perverse nation, among whom ye shine as lights in the world." (Philippians 2.)

Sometimes we must "suffer a while" in order to attain humility and allow God to perfect us.

If we continue as "miserable sinners" after the Holy Spirit has entered us, it is because our desires need to be changed or our faith needs to be strengthened.

344.

Holiness is obedience as to our character. Righteousness is obedience in our relations with others.

Holiness is being possessed completely by Christ. It is being filled with Him. It is His holiness in us.

"To me to live *is* Christ."

345.

As our highest objective is to be filled with God—to attain union with Him—we have a test for our every specific act or thought: does it interfere with our being continuously filled with God? Does it interfere with our continuous union with Him?

What would Jesus do? What would Jesus think?

346.

We often think that we have complied with the conditions for rebirth or for the fulness of the spirit before we have really done so.

Our head may be ready, but our heart may not be ripe; or our heart may be ready, and our head may not.

"It is good that a man should both hope and

quietly wait for the salvation of the Lord." (Lamentations 3.)

"In your patience ye shall win your souls." (Luke 21.)

"Evening, morning, and at noon, will I pray." (Psalm 55.)

"Blessed are they that wait for Him." (Isaiah 30.)

"He charged them not to depart from Jerusalem, but to wait for the promise of the Father." (Acts 1.)

347.

We can find God, be born anew, and receive the fulness of the Holy Spirit by appealing directly to Him.

When He knows that we are ready to abandon that which we are as natural men, He reveals Himself to us. We become conscious of His presence within us, suddenly or gradually.

If we have the humility to realize our own inadequacy and open wide the door to Him by trusting Him completely, we are given an influx of understanding, love and power.

We must never lose sight of the fact we have these only because we have Him.

PART XIV.

348.

"They seek me . . .

Wherefore have we fasted say they . . .

Is not this the fast that I have chosen? to loose the bands of wickedness . . . to deal . . . bread to the hungry? . . .

Behold, the Lord's hand is not shortened, that it cannot save . . .

But your iniquities have separated between you and your God, and your sins have hid His face from you." (Isaiah 58-9.)

349.

We must all:

Ask God to show us ourselves as He sees us.

Hate our nature and give it over to die.

Receive the risen Christ to possess us and fill us.

350.

A general cannot lead his army to success unless his men unquestioningly obey all orders which he gives them. They are most apt to be successful when they are filled with his spirit and love him.

God cannot fulfill His plans for us unless His Spirit has entire possession of us.

We are blameless in His eyes when we have given Him complete possession. "As many as are led by the Spirit of God, these are sons of God."

351.

When we have abandoned our wills, and His will is operating in us, nothing is impossible.

Believe, trust, pray and fast.

With Him, we have "boldness to enter into the holiest." (Hebrews 10.)

352.

We must not "divide" the Cross. It represents both the old and the new covenants.

We are saved by the blood of the lamb *if* we walk with Him to the end. We are *salvable* by the blood.

We cannot accept the atonement if we do not accept the risen Saviour.

353.

We "cleanse ourselves" by letting God do it. *"If we walk in the light,* as He is in the light, the blood of Jesus Christ cleanseth from all sin."

Christ sanctified Himself. We are sanctified by Him, through the offering of His body. (Hebrews 10.)

"The very God of peace sanctify you wholly."

Our salvation is easy for us because it cost God so much.

It is easy for us to be pharisaical about our motives. There is no reason why we should not expect a reward for walking with God, although such expectation becomes subordinated as we abide fully in Him.

"The search for earthly *happiness*, the sense that happiness and goodness naturally and appropriately go together is never going to be eradicated from the life and soul of man.

"The craving for celestial *bliss* will always make one of the deepest passions of the heart which believes in eternity at all.

"The ambition for *character* must forever be the mainspring of much of the noblest of human action.

But the first will be kept from running wild into a mere hunt for luxury, and the second from filling life with unreality and other worldliness, and the third from corrupting into morbid self-consciousness, only as they all are surrounded and commanded by the great unselfish wish to glorify God and to serve fellowman." (Phillips Brooks.)

"To him that overcometh will I give to eat of the tree of life." (Revelations 2.)

"To him that overcometh will I grant to sit with me in my throne, even as I also overcame, and am set down with my Father in His throne." (Revelations 3.)

We do not overcome the world when we flee from it. Almost any ship will ride the water if it is safe in a harbor.

We can develop character by contacts: humility through humiliation, virtue by overcoming temptation, and faith by overcoming that which makes us skeptical.

We overcome the world when we become so distrustful of self, that we give ourselves over to the rule of God.

"What God commands and demands of us, He will Himself work within us . . . Let Him overcome the world for you." (Murray.)

357.

The real Christian is not an anemic man with one foot in the grave.

He is not an innocent man without enough vitality to be bad.

The real Christian is one who has allowed Christ to overcome his old nature.

358.

The spiritual welfare of thousands may hang upon the willingness of one man to make a complete surrender.

359.

We fulfill the conditions for success in our ministry:

1. When we have no unforgiven conscious or unconscious sin—voluntary or involuntary.

2. When we have surrendered all and given God possession of us.

3. When we are identified with the spirit of others by love, and have prayed that their minds and hearts will be opened to receive Him.

4. When we tell them about Jesus: tell them about that which He has done for us, and that which He will do for us.

360.

To God we are either enlisted or not enlisted,—obedient or not obedient.

He looks through our great or little sins to the fact of our surrender or lack of it.

Sins may be small to us but there is no difference to God. They are all disobedience.

361.

"It is the will of God that every one of His children should live entirely and unceasingly under the control of the Holy Spirit.

"Without being filled with the Spirit, it is utterly impossible that an individual Christian or a church can ever live or work as God desires.

"Everywhere and in everything we see the proofs, in the life and experiences of Christians, that this blessing is but little enjoyed in the Church, and, alas! is but little sought for.

"This blessing is prepared for us and God waits to bestow it. Our faith may expect it with the greatest confidence.

"The great hindrance in the way is that the self-life, and the world, which uses it for its own service and pleasure, usurp the place that Christ ought to occupy.

"We cannot be filled with the Spirit until we are prepared to yield ourselves to be led by the Lord Jesus to forsake and sacrifice everything for this pearl of great price." (Murray.)

362.

The faith of Abraham was counted for righteousness.

Solomon asked for wisdom, and other things were added unto him.

Humility, obedience, faith, understanding, love and purity are all parts of the "leaven" that "leavens the whole lump."

If we have humility, the others follow.

An influx of any one adds to the strength of the whole.

They do not come to us because of our scholarship.

They do not come to us because of the length of our service.

They flow into us according to the depth of our surrender.

363.

Faith is opening the door so that Light can come in and shine. It is opening our intellect and heart to Truth.

Faith opens the door so that God can operate through us. He wants us to let Him do great things through us.

364.

When we have believed in the whole gospel—have made a full surrender—have found God and been filled with Him, we *are:*

"Witnesses unto Him"—"good Samaritans."

Used to bring others to Him.

If we are not these things we are only nominal Christians, and are damaging the cause of Christ by giving others a false impression of Christianity.

When we do not wholly believe in the claims and promises of Jesus, and do not wholly walk with Him, we are very likely "soft-soaping" ourselves and others into "the ditch."

365.

God's Holy Spirit, working in us, uses us to draw others to Him.

We are expected in our own persons to reveal the Son of God in us to others. "It pleased God . . . To reveal His Son in me that I might preach him among the heathen." (Galatians 1.)

366.

We must consent to the extinction of all of our own lanterns before the Light will shine for us and in us.

When we are filled with Light, the Light convicts the world of its darkness.

When we walk in our own light, and rely on our own power to influence others, we are soon exhausted spiritually, mentally and physically.

When we walk in His Light and allow Him to flow through us, we are continuously renewed.

Mountains are not removed by strong men. They are removed by God through the meek.

God needs us to bring others to Him.

It is often difficult for unregenerate men to "tune in" with God.

When we are manifestations of Love, we are like a "local station", and men, women and children may be able to tune in with us before they tune in with God.

Men believe in a Redeemer when they meet those whom He has redeemed. They believe in Christ when they see those whom Love has transformed.

368.

When we become filled with God—like Jesus— "power goes out from us" without effort on our part.

God *is* love. Love *is* power.

All our needs are supplied when we are filled with God.

We need only concentrate upon giving Him every part of ourselves so that He can fill us.

369.

There are some who do not like the idea of God using them as a channel. They "do not want to lose their personality."

Did Dwight Moody or Phillips Brooks lose his personality?

We might never have heard of St. Paul if he had not consented to be used as a channel. It was when he ceased resisting that the love, power and wisdom of God flowed through him.

It is when the Living Water pours through us that we have power. It is the Life which is in the Vine that is creative. Only as channels can we produce fruit.

370.

The natural man *cannot* serve God. He is at enmity against God consciously or unconsciously. (Romans 8.)

Natural man "lusteth against the Spirit." He is "accursed." In him "dwells no good thing." He "never can be" co-operative with God. (Romans 8.)

That is why he must be "given over to die."

371.

If we are proud of our strong wills, our reasoning, our skill, or our experience, it is keeping us from being filled with God.

Our natural gifts may charm and stir people, but they do not move them—do not make them act.

372.

When shall we fast? How shall we fast?

"Ye have not eaten bread, neither have ye drunk wine or strong drink: that ye might know that I am the Lord your God." (Deuteronomy 29.)

"Butter and honey shall he eat, that he may know to refuse the evil, and choose the good." (Isaiah 7.)

"This kind goeth not out but by prayer and fasting." (Matthew 17.)

PART XV.

373.

We are not Christians because we "join church," read the Bible, pray or take communion. We are not Christians because we sign our name to a creed.

We are not Christians because we do not use alcohol or tobacco, or do not play cards, go to the theatre or dance.

We are not Christians because we give money to charity or do good works. We are not Christians although we give all our goods to the poor.

We are not Christians although we have an intellectual belief in the deity of Jesus, in His virgin birth, that we are saved by His blood, and that He arose from the dead and has ascended into heaven.

374.

We must be able to witness as to our first hand experiences with God. "Woe unto the foolish prophets, that follow their own spirit, and have seen nothing." (Ezekiel 13.)

We often say: have we got *it?*

We should say: have we got *Him?*

More accurately: *has He got us?*

Have we had experiences with Him?

More accurately: have we had *transforming* experiences with Him?

Are we abiding in Him?

We must know "where we are, and why" if we would help others.

375.

Many ministers say that less than ten per cent of our congregations are converted. If this is correct, much of our preaching and writing is over the heads of our listeners and readers.

If we assume that our audience has found God when ninety per cent of them have not found Him, we are failing to deliver the message for which there is the most need. We are "offering to the blind what is profitable only for the seeing." (Bowen.)

376.

When we have not found God we sometimes substitute church membership for Him.

Formalism takes the place of worship, because we cannot worship the God whom we have not found.

Our ceremonies conceal our separation from God.

Sometimes we substitute social service, or Bible classes or social clubs.

That which should be only a *means* is regarded as an *end*. All church associations should be scouting organizations for Christ.

Christianity is not hereditary. If the world should be brought to Christ in this generation, it would be necessary to convert it again in the next generation. All men must be "born again."

When we understand this, we comprehend why the *institution* deteriorates so easily. It is only as Christian as the individuals who compose it at the time.

Jesus has given us His judgment in one sentence upon nominal Christianity—upon those who profess faith, but do not commit themselves and all that they have to Him: "I will spue thee out of my mouth." (Revelation 3.)

Many church members have accepted forgiveness, but are living under the old covenant—the law. They are trying to improve their old nature instead of letting God give them a new nature. Consequently they are solemn and discouraged.

They are not "singing for joy of heart."

Although they may not realize it, there are some "churches" which are really teaching Hellenism. They are advertising from the pulpit that they have nothing to offer that cannot be obtained elsewhere.

They are preaching a "religion" that does not work. They are holding up gods which do not exist.

They are teaching reason, common-sense, self-reliance, or partial self-reliance instead of faith and entire dependence on God.

"They make you vain: they speak a vision of their own heart, and not out of the mouth of the Lord." (Jeremiah 23.)

381.

There are churches here and there which persuade themselves that they are fruitless because they are "living in a Godless generation"—in the midst of a Sahara Desert—of stony and thorny ground. That would be a dark picture! It is largely untrue.

Thousands are consciously searching for God. They are going to halls and "centers" hoping to find an answer to their problems. They feel there must be an answer to the cruelty, fears, poverty and insecurity of mankind. There is developing a great thirst for God.

The harvest is plenteous.

382.

Wherever there is satisfaction with the condition of the church, it is indeed dead. The self-satisfied are furthermost from God. We should pity them and pray for them: they have a long journey ahead of them.

God's plan is to work through us. The branch and the Vine need each other.

The Church of Christ should be so perfectly built that it would look like one stone. No one who understands what judgment means would dare to allow personal ambition to interfere with this.

383.

A filled church does not mean that Christ is there. Men and women are apt to flock to those who teach that which they wish to believe. Such churches are our worst enemies. They are wolves in sheep's clothing. We would be better off with their opposition than with their alliance.

"The time will come when they will not endure sound doctrine; but after their own lusts shall they heap to themselves teachers, having itching ears;

"And they shall turn away their ears from the truth, and shall be turned unto fables." (2 Timothy 4.)

Nevertheless, if a church is dead—if men, women and children are not being converted—we can know that Christ is not there. He is Life.

384.

"Religious education" alone will not give us understanding. Only the pure in heart can perceive Truth.

We must surrender to God, and be willing to let Him make us all that He tells us we should be, before Truth is accessible for us.

Understanding can only come when the Spirit of Truth is in us.

A man may accept the doctrine of the incarnation and atonement as authoritative, yet have seen nothing.

No one is fully equipped for the ministry until he has been born again and has received the fulness of the Holy Spirit.

Scholarship is a valuable accessory. It is a background—not a foundation.

Not by might, nor by ability, nor by activity, nor by education, "but by My Spirit, saith the Lord of Hosts." (Zechariah 4.)

"I think I speak not too strongly when I say that a church in the land without the Spirit of God is rather a curse than a blessing. If you have not the Spirit of God, Christian worker, remember that you stand in somebody else's way; you are as a tree bearing no fruit standing where another fruitful tree might grow." (Spurgeon.)

Denominational differences often arise because we think that the will of God for us should be a rule for all men.

The deeper differences which cut across denominational differences are often only the varying degrees of progress toward the full revelation. Some of us are apt to pray: "God lead me to the truth, but do not tell me *this* or *that* because I will not believe it."

Our doctrines change as we receive more of Truth.

"As Moses lifted up the serpent in the wilderness, even so must the Son of man be lifted up." (John 3.)

"When ye have lifted up the Son of man, then shall ye know that I am He." (John 8.)

"I, if I be lifted up from the earth will draw all men unto me." (John 12.)

"Christ sent me . . . to preach the gospel." (1 Corinthians 1.)

"We preach Christ crucified." (1 Corinthians 1.)

"He preached unto them Jesus and the resurrection." (Acts 17.)

"I have fully preached the gospel of Christ." (Romans 15.)

389.

"My speech and my preaching was not with enticing words of man's wisdom, but in demonstration of the Spirit, and of power: that your faith should not stand in the wisdom of men, but in the power of God." (St. Paul.)

We *must* go to the Source. We must take time to be alone with God.

390.

There are several snares in preaching and teaching. They make it difficult for us to remain humble.

They also tend to make us satisfy ourselves by talking. By expression we easily exhaust our capacity for action.

391.

The command is that we glorify God. We are not doing it unless we are bearing fruit.

This is the test which Jesus tells us we must all apply to ourselves. He says: "Herein is my Father glorified that ye bear much fruit; so that ye be my disciples." If He is not converting men through us we can know we are not right with Him.

The bringing of people to Him is the test He gives us as to whether we are abiding in Him. It is the ultimate test as to whether we are *in* Him, *like* Him, and as to the soundness of our doctrine.

392.

It is often said that revival meetings are too emotional.

It is true that we do not find God through our emotions: but no one can meet his Creator without emotion.

The fault is more apt to be in the apathy of the church to which the convert goes for fellowship in walking with God.

393.

A few centuries ago there was a religious revolution which emphasized the forgiveness of sins for those who received Christ. It emphasized *pardon*.

We need a revival that will also emphasize the fact that the hand of God is outstretched to lift—that Christ is living and is eager to enter us and exercise His *power* in us. It is when we experience this that we "sing for joy of heart."

"My son was dead, and is alive again; he was lost, and is found. And they began to be merry.

. . . It was meet that we should make merry, and be glad." (Luke 15.)

394.

The Church of Christ is composed of those who are possessed by Christ.

It is composed of those who have enlisted in the Kingdom of God.

It exists within the organized church and outside of it.

395.

The Church of Christ consists of those who keep His commandments. "By this shall all men know that ye are my disciples if ye have love one to another."

"Christians are known by their resemblance to Christ." (Bowen.)

396.

The Church of Christ is composed of those who have received the Holy Spirit—the Spirit of Adoption, and have been born of God, so that they have the right to call Him, Father.

Do we hate the nature with which we were born? Have we given it over to be "crucified with Christ"? Have we been "planted in the likeness of His death"?

Have we separated ourselves from all worldliness? Have we surrendered everything?

Have we had a *transforming* experience? Has Christ entered into us and *filled* us? Do we love God and our neighbor? Are we devoted to Jesus Christ and to His plans for man?

To ministers, Andrew Murray says:

"Have you ever earnestly thought over why it is that you have a salary and a parsonage, and are set free from the need of following earthly business? It is for nothing else than that you should continue in prayer and the ministry of the Word. That will be your wisdom and your power. That will be the secret of a blessed service of the Gospel . . .

" 'It is not reason,' said Peter, 'that we should leave the Word of God, and serve tables.' For that work deacons were chosen. And this word of Peter serves for all time and for all who are set apart as ministers."

398.

"Intercessory prayer is our main work." (Oswald Chambers.)

"It is the highest office of the will of man." (Murray.)

It is for the purpose of bringing others into the Kingdom.

It is for the purpose of learning God's will as to that which He would have us do for others.

399.

We do not understand just how intercessory prayer works, but we know that it is in this way that God works through us and upon the conscious and subconscious minds of others.

We also know that when we efface ourselves and

"pray in the Holy Spirit"—allow the Holy Spirit in us to do the praying—that by listening, we learn the will of God regarding others.

400.

Intercessory prayer is the *condition we must fulfill* if we are to be used to save others.

God operates through faith. We need only obey as the Israelites did when they looked on the brazen serpent, or as Naaman did when he immersed himself seven times in the Jordan.

We must *obey even though we do not understand.*

401.

Christian fellowship is meeting at the feet of Jesus.

402.

We should all be "one body." We should all work for unity.

Our most efficient work is in bringing others into the Kingdom.

If men are really brought to Christ there *is* unity.

When all men become God-centered, they meet at the center. They *are* all parts of one body.

403.

It takes many wore words to tell what the gospel is *not,* than to tell what the gospel *is.*

The gospel is:

If we let Him, the Holy Spirit—the Spirit of Jesus and God—Christ, Himself—God, Himself—will enter us and make us like Himself.

If we are willing that the "old" man shall die, Christ will take his place. He will *identify* Himself with the "new" man.

404.

Jesus effaced Himself, and lived by the Father.

He fed on the Father. The Father was His wisdom and power. The Father's will was His will.

It was not Jesus the man that did God's works. It was God in Jesus that did the works.

Similarly, we must feed upon and live with Christ by and in the Father, as He lives by and in the Father.

We must efface ourselves and let God, in Christ, through the Holy Spirit, think and act in us.

405.

We are saved by the precious blood of Jesus Christ. "When I see the blood, I will pass over you, and the plagues shall not be upon you to destroy you." (Exodus 12.)

Through Christ—because of Him—we can enter the Holy of Holies.

Through Him—because of Him—we can be united with God—"hid with Christ in God."

"I in them, and Thou in me that they may be made perfect in One." (John 17.)

May the Word of God come unto all of us and may He put it in our hearts to pray:

Almighty God, we confess our unbelief. We confess our indifference. We confess our corruption.

Many times we have sinned against Thee and Thou hast forgiven us.

Our Father, we repent again and humbly beseech Thy forgiveness.

We realize our complete dependence on Thee. Put it into our minds and hearts to comply with the conditions so that Thou canst revive us, and cause us to walk with Christ in Thee.

Father, help us to realize our sinful nature and to keep it crucified. Help us to trust Thee for this.

Give us the faith to realize that Thou art in us, and that Thou wilt perfect us in every good work to do Thy will: that Thou wilt make us unblameable in holiness.

Help us to gird up our loins like men realizing we can do all things through Thee who worketh in us.

Possess us so completely that we will sing for joy of heart.